FLIP THE SCRIPT

Published by SuccessBooks®, Lake Mary, FL.

SuccessBooks® is a registered trademark.

ISBN: 979-8-9918645-5-8
LCCN: 2025909985

This publication is designed to provide accurate and authoritative information with regard to the subject matter covered. It is sold with the understanding that the publisher is not engaged in rendering legal, accounting, or other professional advice. If legal advice or other expert assistance is required, the services of a competent professional should be sought. The opinions expressed by the authors in this book are not endorsed by SuccessBooks® and are the sole responsibility of the author rendering the opinion.

Most SuccessBooks® titles are available at special quantity discounts for bulk purchases for sales promotions, premiums, fundraising, and educational use. Special versions or book excerpts can also be created to fit specific needs.

For more information, please write:

SuccessBooks®
3415 W. Lake Mary Blvd. #950370
Lake Mary, FL 32795
or call 1.877.261.4930

Visit us online at: www.CelebrityPressPublishing.com.

FLIP THE SCRIPT

SCRIPT

USING TACTICAL EMPATHY
TO TURN TOUGH TALKS INTO
BREAKTHROUGH RESULTS

SUCCESS
BOOKS®
Lake Mary, FL

CONTENTS

CHAPTER 1

FLIPPING THE SCRIPT THROUGH THE POWER OF TACTICAL EMPATHY

By Chris Voss

Most people approach negotiation as if it is a battle of logic, a contest of pressure, or the deployment of ultimatums. They arm themselves with facts and brace for a struggle. These are common tactics.

Using common tactics makes you common.

The real secret to power negotiations comes from understanding the emotions driving the other side's actions, and then articulating that understanding. Power negotiations come from power relationships. And nothing creates power relationships like flipping the script through the use of tactical empathy.

This chapter highlights three pivotal scenarios where tactical empathy made all the difference. First, we'll step into a high-stakes hostage situation where two bank robbers held innocent people's lives in their hands, and how careful listening and emotional validation turned a volatile situation into a peaceful resolution.

Then we'll explore a professional negotiation, where a job candidate facing an underwhelming offer used tactical empathy to transform it into an incredible deal. Finally, we'll revisit one of the toughest cases I ever faced—a hostage situation in the Phillippines where a man's life hung in the balance, and how understanding human emotions ultimately led to his safe return.

In each of these stories, success didn't come from force, pressure, or ultimatums. It came from making the other side *feel* heard and in control. That's the essence of tactical empathy. By the end of this chapter, you'll see how it can transform not just negotiations but any conversation, even where the stakes are high.

THE BANK HOSTAGE STANDOFF

One of the most striking examples of tactical empathy in action comes from my time as an FBI hostage negotiator. Two bank robbers found themselves trapped inside a bank with hostages. The criminals were panicked, unpredictable, and armed. A typical approach to a standoff like this might be to show force, demand surrender, threaten consequences, or attempt to outmaneuver the perpetrators by some sort of lie.

Instead, I understood that flipping the script meant that I needed to *listen* to recognize and then call out (by labeling) their fears. I needed them to *feel heard*, not cornered.

Questions where you are trying to get someone to say yes make people feel cornered. And *actually* understanding them is not directly correlated to them *actually feeling* understood.

By my expressing tactical empathy, they felt I understood their situation—not in a way that excused their actions but in a way that made them inclined to trust me, and then be influenced by me.

I used tone, patience, and carefully chosen words to establish rapport. Rather than issuing commands, I asked, "How is everyone inside?" This *calibrated ("What?" or "How?") question* caused him to realize that it wasn't only the hostages I was concerned for but him as well.

From there I expanded my approach by incorporating *mirroring* and *labeling*. "It seems like this isn't what you planned for" is an example.

When one of the robbers said, "You chased my driver away," I mirrored his words: "We chased your driver away?" This simple technique triggered him to continue talking, revealing information he had planned to hold back.

By acknowledging/labeling fears, I defused tension. The more he spoke, the more I understood his motivations. He wasn't just trying to escape; he was overwhelmed and scared of making a mistake that could get him badly hurt or killed. By maintaining a calm and understanding tone, I led him away from his defensive posture and into a mindset where he was open to guidance.

As the standoff continued, I introduced more *calibrated questions* to guide toward a peaceful resolution. "What's stopping you from coming out?" I asked. This small but powerful question made him divert from fear and moved him to reflect on his predicament, giving him the feeling of control.

By shifting the focus from demands, I encouraged the robbers to see me as an ally rather than an adversary. Through the constant use of a soft, patient voice instead of a harsh or authoritative one—I reassured him on a deeper level that safety was the primary concern.

As the negotiation reached its final stages, *dynamic silence* (pausing strategically after key moments to let words sink in) was used. Silence can be incredibly uncomfortable, compelling the other party to fill the void. In the end, after hours of careful engagement, the robbers surrendered without harm to the hostages. Tactical empathy had transformed a potentially deadly situation into a controlled, peaceful outcome. This experience reinforced what I have always believed: The key to negotiation is not force but understanding.

THE COMMON MISTAKES IN TOUGH CONVERSATIONS

Most people default to logic in high-stakes conversations, believing that if they present the right facts, the other person will see reason. This approach fails because logic is like beauty—it's in the eye of the beholder. All people make their "logical" decisions from their cornerstones of values **and** gut instinct.

Emotions drive people, and ignoring them only creates resistance.

Another common mistake is using "leverage," or pressure. Whether it's a boss telling an employee, "You have to improve, or you're fired," or a negotiator saying, "Take the deal, or we walk," pressure makes people defensive. It triggers their instinct to push back or shut down.

Ultimatums are another error. They eliminate flexibility and, rather than compelling cooperation, often lead to worse outcomes. I have learned that by creating a sense of partnership rather than confrontation, better outcomes are revealed.

REVERSING A JOB OFFER REJECTION

This was not because we pushed harder but because we let them feel in control.

The job offer came in. And it was insulting.

The candidate had experience, a proven track record. The number they offered was nowhere near what he expected.

Most people counter with demands: "I need at least…" "This isn't competitive." "I can't accept less than…"

That never creates the best outcome because the second you start fighting over a number, you lock yourself into a battle where someone has to lose. And it's never a great start to a job if either of you feels it began with a loss.

Instead, I had him shift the conversation.

Rather than rejecting the offer, I coached him to use a series of no-oriented questions to make the hiring manager rethink their offer. The questions had to be delivered with genuine curiosity and included:

- "Are you saying I'm the wrong person for the job?"
- "Do you want me to be so anxious about my compensation that I fail?"

- "Are you saying there are other people you'd rather hire?"
- "Are you saying you don't believe in my future here?"

While these clearly feel to you like scary confrontational questions, everyone feels safe and secure when they say no. It's a Pavlovian response. The key is to ask them politely, gently, and with genuine curiosity. Genuine curiosity is impossible to resist.

Now, instead of defending their number, the manager *felt* in complete control.

Boom. The door opened, and they made a much higher offer.

A HOSTAGE NEGOTIATION GONE WRONG—THEN RIGHT

One of the toughest negotiations I ever faced came during a kidnapping case in the Phillippines. An American businessman had been taken by a ruthless kidnapper. When it first began, I had the sense that we were communicating with the kidnapper's boss instead of the usual henchman in the kidnapping gang whose job it was to handle the negotiations.

What were the clues I saw? The kidnapper's overuse of plural pronouns, intentionally shifting importance away from himself. The mark of a shrewd decision-maker is to lessen his own importance to avoid being cornered into a commitment.

As it turned out, he wasn't just the boss. He was a lone kidnapper and a serial killer. This combination is the only one I ever encountered in my entire career.

The kidnapper made his demands clear: Pay a daily "fee" just to keep the hostage alive while the kidnapper researched the family to calculate a ransom, or the hostage would suffer the consequences.

This wasn't just about money; it was about survival. The hostage's family was in a state of panic, desperate to give in to the demands. But as I knew from experience, paying too quickly would only invite more danger—it would signal to the kidnappers that they could keep pushing for more. Instead, I had to slow things down and create a sense of control where we had none.

The secret to gaining the upper hand in a negotiation is to give the illusion of control.

Calibrated questions give the illusion of control. These are almost exclusively "What?" and "How?" questions. They *feel* deferential to the person being asked them. People love to be asked what to do and how to do it.

At the same time, they tend to both constrain the thinking of the other side within specific parameters. They require in-depth thinking to solve. Thus, they steer the conversation away from threats and toward collaboration.

So instead of reacting to their threats, I (and my team) coached the family member talking to the kidnapper to ask, "How do we know that if we pay, he will be OK?"

We did a great job of coaching the family representative. But even more importantly he was extremely coachable. Finally on his own, he created this phenomenal calibrated question: "When we run out of money paying the daily rate, what's going to happen?"

The kidnapper hesitated and said, "It will be all right." At this moment, the momentum completely changed to our favor, as the kidnapper had just promised (without realizing it) to not harm the hostage.

Slowly, the conversation had turned. The kidnapper started seeing us as human, not just as adversaries. Instead of issuing more threats, he engaged in problem-solving.

The ransom was negotiated down to a fraction of the original demand. Then, in the final stages, the businessman was rescued! Great negotiation creates great outcomes, not all of them planned for. Engage in a great process, and let great things happen.

THE SKILLS BEHIND TACTICAL EMPATHY

Over the years, I have refined specific skills that make tactical empathy so effective. These include *mirroring, labeling, calibrated questions, tonality, no-oriented questions,* and *dynamic silence—* each playing a crucial role in disarming resistance and fostering trust.

- **Mirroring:** One of the simplest yet most effective tools, mirroring involves repeating the last few words the other person says. It encourages them to elaborate and feel understood without forcing the conversation but guiding it gently.

- **Labeling:** This technique involves naming the emotions you observe or sense in the other person. When I say, "It sounds like you're feeling frustrated about this decision," it makes them feel understood and lowers their defenses.

- **Calibrated questions:** Instead of asking yes/no questions, I use open-ended questions designed to keep the other person engaged. Questions such as, "How do you see this playing out?" or "What's the biggest challenge you're facing?" encourage them to share their perspective in a way that feels safe and productive.

- **Tonality:** The way you say something matters at least as much as the words you choose. I consciously adjust my tone and inflection to create calm, understanding, and encouragement. This helps them feel trust.

- **No-oriented questions:** People feel safe and secure when they say no. It's a counterintuitive secret that works like a magic wand.

- **Dynamic silence:** Sometimes the most powerful tool is saying nothing at all. By allowing strategic pauses, I give the other party space to process their thoughts and often encourage them to reveal more than they initially intended.

THE TAKEAWAY

Each of the three scenarios in this chapter demonstrates the profound impact of tactical empathy in high-stakes negotiations. Whether defusing a dangerous hostage standoff, transforming an insulting job offer into a beneficial deal, or securing the safe release of a kidnapped businessman, the same core principles applied: listening, recognizing emotions, and guiding the conversation toward a mutually beneficial outcome.

In the bank hostage situation, tactical empathy allowed me to disarm volatile criminals not by force but by making them feel heard and in control. Instead of escalating the confrontation, I guided them toward peaceful surrender.

The job-offer negotiation highlighted a common pitfall: reacting to a low offer with demands rather than strategic curiosity. By shifting the conversation through no-oriented questions, the candidate avoided direct confrontation, prompting the employer to reconsider and ultimately sweeten the deal.

The high-stakes kidnapping case in the Phillippines illustrated how tactical empathy works even in life-or-death situations. By steering the conversation with calibrated questions, I shifted the negotiation dynamic. The result? A rescue enabled by getting the kidnapper to feel in control and drop his guard.

Tactical empathy is not about manipulation or being overly accommodating—it's about understanding what truly drives human decisions.

Tactical empathy is not about being soft. It's about recognizing that people need to feel heard before they will listen. By understanding what drives the other person, by using tone, patience, and well-placed words, you can disarm resistance and build trust in any high-stakes conversation.

Mastering these techniques can help in negotiations, conflict resolution, leadership, and even personal relationships. By fostering connection rather than opposition, tactical empathy creates opportunities for collaboration, helping all parties find better outcomes. Whether in a bank standoff, a boardroom, or everyday life, the principles of tactical empathy remain the same: slow down, listen, label, and guide.

Those who master these skills can turn adversaries into allies and obstacles into solutions, proving that the most effective negotiators are not those who demand but those who demonstrate they understand.

About Chris

Chris Voss is the best-selling author of *Never Split the Difference*, a former lead international FBI kidnapping negotiator, and the CEO and founder of The Black Swan Group.

During his twenty-four-year career with the FBI, Chris served as the FBI's hostage negotiation representative for the National Security Council's Hostage Working Group and has represented the US at two international conferences. He's been recognized for a number of awards, including the Attorney General's Award, and the FBI Agents Association Award for Distinguished and Exemplary Service. He has received negotiation training from the FBI, Scotland Yard, and Harvard Law School.

Since retiring from the FBI, Chris has earned his master's in public administration from Harvard University and taught at a number of esteemed institutions, including the University of Southern California Marshall School of Business, Georgetown University, Harvard University, Northwestern University, the IMD Business School in Lausanne, Switzerland, and the Goethe Business School in Frankfurt, Germany.

Following the success of his book *Never Split the Difference*, Chris coauthored a book with real estate guru Steve Shull, *The Full Fee Agent*, which provides practical and skillful negotiation techniques for real estate agents—both experienced and expert. Chris has been featured on podcasts and media outlets such as *Time* magazine, CNN, CNBC, the Lex Fridman podcast Inc., and others.

His company, The Black Swan Group, established in 2008, aims at providing negotiation coaching for professionals all over the world through corporate and individual coaching, as well as live events.

When he isn't coaching or giving keynote speeches, Chris is passionate about learning, working out, reading, and spending time with his family. He currently lives in Las Vegas.

To connect with Chris and his company, you can go to blackswanltd.com. You can also follow him on LinkedIn and Instagram.

CHAPTER 2

THROUGH THE WRONG DOOR

By Caleb Summerfelt

"**C**ome eat!"

Mom called from the kitchen. Between me and my seat at the table was a doorway. Just one, right? At least that's what everyone else saw. But for me, there were dozens. Doorways stacked on top of each other. Finding the real one was a gamble every single time. The doorways twisted and shifted like some weird optical illusion, until I had no clue which one was real. I'd take a step, then another, trusting my intuition more than my eyes. My foot hit a wall that wasn't supposed to be there, and my shoulder smacked into a frame I couldn't even see. It happened over and over—until, eventually, I tripped my way through the real doorway, collecting one more bruise for the day.

That was pretty much my childhood—bumping into walls, tripping over things, and way too many trips to the ER. My first memories aren't about bedtime stories or playgrounds. They're about bright hospital lights, cold antiseptic wipes, and doctors muttering about how I managed to split my head open this time.

Everything I looked at came with extras—extra letters, extra numbers, extra doorways, extra faces. Some days I'd see five of everything. Other days it was closer to a dozen. Even writing my own name was a mess. The letters wouldn't sit still, and by the time I finished, it looked as if I'd written across half the page. Reading? Forget it. One sentence would stretch into a dozen, and the words wouldn't stop moving long enough for me to figure out what they said.

I didn't know this was abnormal.

How would I know something was wrong? I didn't know what "normal" looked like. To me, the way I saw the world was just…the way it was. I didn't have the words to explain that what I saw wasn't what everyone else saw. All I knew was that I couldn't read right, couldn't write correctly, and couldn't walk across a room without crashing into something. Teachers said I wasn't trying hard enough. The other kids called me stupid, and the school decided I belonged in special ed. The first time I saw the alphabet the way everyone else did, I actually laughed. It looked wrong— stiff, stuck in place, almost broken. I'd spent my whole life chasing letters that wouldn't sit still, and now here they were, just sitting there like they were glued to the page. No wonder reading never made sense to me before. Nobody else saw what I saw. Nobody else lived in that jumbled-up, constantly moving world. Nobody— except Mom.

Mom didn't just notice something was off—she *believed* my descriptions. Long before any doctor gave it a name, she knew I wasn't lazy or stupid. She knew I was fighting a battle nobody else could see. And that belief would change everything. Mom wasn't a doctor, but she knew something was wrong, and she wasn't about to let anyone brush me off. She started digging, reading everything she could, and taking me to appointment after appointment until we finally found a doctor who got it. Turns out I had a rare visual and processing disorder that made me see extra copies of everything. But the real lesson wasn't just the diagnosis; it was watching *how* she got people to listen. She didn't yell or demand. She made them see my world through my eyes. That's the first time I saw tactical empathy in action, and I never forgot it.

Once we finally had a diagnosis, I had to start over—relearning how to read and write in high school, right alongside everyone else who already had it figured out. That's when I really started to understand what is now called tactical empathy. The world wasn't going to adapt for me—I had to find a way to make people *under-stand* what I was going through so I could succeed.

That lesson stuck. Every time someone questioned me, under-estimated me, or flat-out doubted I belonged, I leaned on empathy to turn it around. Just as my mother had worked tirelessly to make doctors understand that I was different, I would have to work tire-lessly to help the world understand that my difference was my superpower.

Controlling the Narrative

The first time I walked in and saw my architectural model trashed, I just stood there, trying to process it. Hours of work—gone. Pieces scattered across the floor like someone's idea of a joke. I wasn't sure whether to be mad, hurt, or just stunned that anyone cared enough to hate me that much.

Architecture school wasn't exactly friendly territory. The pro-gram was meant to be intense—they set the bar high and expected you to hit it, no excuses. The other students made it clear I didn't belong, but pressure like that didn't really rattle me. I had already spent my whole life figuring out how to work around obstacles other people couldn't even see. While others panicked under pres-sure, I had already trained myself to approach problems differ-ently and work around obstacles.

They didn't like that I could figure things out a little faster than they could, especially with a learning difference. They also didn't like the accommodations I was granted to help work around my disability because they thought it gave me some kind of edge. They saw it as an unfair advantage, oblivious to the reality that school would have been impossible to me without these minor conces-sions. They didn't stop at words. They crushed my models and trashed my work, keyed my truck, and broke into my apartment. And one day—right in class—someone stabbed me.

I had every reason to be suspicious of them. But here's the thing: Anger wasn't going to fix anything. It wouldn't get my work back. It wouldn't make them respect me. I had a decision to make: let them win, or write my own story. So I flipped the script—for all of us.

Tactical empathy isn't about letting people off the hook. It's about helping them see something they've never had to think about before—and once they see it, they can't ignore it. That's how you change the story. My classmates did not get it, and my professors questioned the disability. One of my professors figured I was just another kid trying to play the sympathy card. I bombed the first quiz in his class—which didn't make sense since I usually pulled top grades. When I asked to talk to him after class, I could see it right away—he didn't believe me. "I know you say you have a disability," he said, "but I've heard that before, and most of the time, it's just an excuse to get out of the work." I didn't argue. I said, "Imagine this: You're trying to do a math problem, but every time you look at the numbers, they jump or smear somewhere. Or you're reading a sentence, but the letters keep rearranging themselves before you can even get to the end. How would you handle that?" I saw the shift in his eyes.

For the first time, I wasn't just some kid asking for a break. I was a person with a legitimate concern he'd never thought about. He let me redo the quiz—not for a better grade but just so he could watch how I worked. When I did it aloud, he saw the difference. After that he let me type my exams instead of handwriting them—not because he had to but because he understood. That moment taught me something: People don't resist because they don't care; they resist because they don't *know*. If I could make them see what I saw, I could change their thoughts. If I could flip their script, I could shift their perspective.

Years later, when one of the students who troubled me in school reached out—changed, remorseful—I made the same choice. I listened. I let them explain. And in doing so, they had to confront the truth of their actions. Empathy didn't just change me. It changed them. In order to replace barriers with bridges, I had to guide the people around me from frustration to understanding. I had to show *them* empathy before I could expect it in return.

The Obstacle Is, in Fact, the Way

Empathy felt like a dangerous choice when I was surrounded by people who saw my difference as a weakness. The students who destroyed my work, slashed my models, and vandalized my truck weren't just trying to make my life hard—they were trying to erase me. I was told if I could not handle it to withdraw.

And at first, I'll admit, I was angry. And yet in those moments, I had to ask myself, "What if my disability wasn't a setback? What if this was my greatest advantage?" That was the shift that changed everything. Instead of fixating on the hatred thrown my way, I focused on what my disability *gave* me—a different way of seeing the world, a different way of solving problems. While they were focused on tearing me down, I was focused on pushing forward. And then, I realized something even bigger: My disability wasn't a weakness—it was my leverage.

Think about it, every major innovation and every breakthrough starts with someone facing an obstacle others couldn't overcome. What if your biggest struggle is actually your greatest strength waiting to be uncovered? For me, the way my mind processed information—once seen as a defect—became an asset. Where others saw problems, I saw patterns. Where others struggled to think outside the box, I had *never* lived inside the box to begin with. When a project seemed impossible, I broke it apart, analyzed it from unusual angles, and found unusual solutions.

This ability didn't just help me survive architecture school; it shaped my career, my relationships, and my ability to navigate a world not built for people like me. And beyond that it gave me something even more powerful: the ability to help others. Because I knew what it felt like to be dismissed, I made sure others felt seen. Because I knew what it was like to struggle, I made sure others had someone in their corner. Because I knew what it meant to be underestimated, I made sure no one could underestimate *me* again.

Maybe you're facing something right now that feels impossible.

How can you flip it? Maybe you've been told that the way you think, work, or operate in the world isn't "normal." Maybe you've convinced yourself that a challenge in your life is a barrier that will keep you from success. But what if the opposite is true? What if the thing you've always seen as your greatest disadvantage is actually your greatest edge? What if, instead of wishing it away, you *leaned in to it*? I was diagnosed in high school, and in that moment, I had a choice: let this new reality break me, or use it as a tool for growth. I refused to be the victim. I chose growth, and every time I faced resistance, every time someone tried to shut me out, I made a promise to myself: My resilience would speak louder than their hatred ever could. That moment defined me. I didn't need to fight. I could win with *perspective*, with *persistence*, and with an unshakable belief in my own worth. What if the obstacle in front of you isn't there to stop you but to show you the way?

Designing Your Own Destiny

People have told me I should be angry, that I should have held grudges and made sure the people who tried to break me paid for what they did.

But here's the truth: *They didn't win.* They did everything they could to erase me, to make me feel small, to convince me I didn't belong. And yet here I am. I built a career spanning decades, leading innovation in industries where people like me were never expected to succeed. For twenty years I was the chief information officer of a manufacturing company.

When that company sold, I could have seen it as an ending. Instead, I saw an opportunity. I founded NSB Design Works, and Great Bowerbirdling Design, where I lead an incredible team of designers, engineers, and project managers, delivering high-impact solutions across industries. I took my passion for design, problem-solving, and leadership and turned it into something bigger than myself. Looking at giving back, I stepped into service. As the 2023–2024 governor for Rotary International District 5020,

I helped lead initiatives that raised $11.5 million for the Rotary Foundation—real impact, real change. I launched UD5020, a digital platform connecting over ten thousand readers each month through cohesive branding and storytelling. I built this life; *I designed it*—not despite challenges but *because* of them.

Now I find myself at another turning point. The next phase of my life isn't just about my own success—it's about helping others step beyond their challenges and into leadership. It's about helping people design their own destiny, control their own narrative, and redefine what success looks like on their terms, because *that's* what my mother did for me. She saw beyond the labels, the assumptions, and the dismissals. She understood what I needed when no one else did, and she *pushed* until I got help. She showed me that the right support can change a life.

Now I want to be that person for others.

If you're reading this and wondering whether your struggles are a barrier to success, ask yourself this: "What if my different perspective is exactly what the world needs? What if the very thing people told me would hold me back is what will set me apart? What if instead of trying to play by their rules, I create my own?" I was never supposed to succeed by traditional standards. I was an outsider from the beginning—misunderstood, doubted, and underestimated. But I didn't let that stop me. And neither should you.

This isn't just my story—it's a tribute. A tribute to my mother. A tribute to the people who have fought battles no one else can see. A tribute to those who refuse to let their struggles define them. One person made a difference in my life. And now, through this story, I hope to do the same for someone else. Because your contribution matters. Because different perspectives lead to growth. Because at the end of the day we hold the narrative of our personal lives. When the world doesn't make space for you, write your own world and build it on empathy, resilience, and an unwavering faith that your challenges are actually clues to your zone of genius.

About Caleb

Innovator, Leader, and Designer

For over twenty-two years Caleb Summerfelt has combined leadership, innovation and creativity to drive impactful change in technology, branding and design. As a retired CIO, he oversaw critical infrastructure, including network security, phone systems and building automation, while leading product and packaging design, branding initiatives and marketing strategies. His ability to integrate technical expertise with creative vision defined his career, where he consistently delivered innovative solutions and measurable results.

Caleb holds a Bachelor of Science in architecture, a Master of Architecture and a Master of Engineering Technology Management—all from Washington State University. Additionally, he has earned certifications in constraints management, logistics and supply chain management, and project management from Washington State University; has completed the TOCICO Theory of Constraints Strategic Thinking Process Program ("Jonah"); and holds a certificate in AI 360: Advanced AI & Data Science for Business Strategy from Cornell University. His educational background bridges design, technology and leadership, equipping him with the skills to innovate across industries.

After retiring in 2023, Caleb focused his creative energy on leading NSB Design Works and Great Bowerbirdling Design. NSB Design Works specializes in fabrication, engineering and custom metalwork, blending craftsmanship with modern design solutions. Great Bowerbirdling Design focuses on web and graphic design, storytelling and digital media. Through these ventures, Caleb bridges technology, creativity and precision, helping businesses and organizations develop compelling brands, streamline operations and achieve measurable success.

Caleb's passion for service is evident in his leadership within Rotary International. As the 2023–2024 District 5020 governor for one of the largest districts in the world, he led initiatives that inspired and raised $11.5 million for the Rotary Foundation. His dedication to service, storytelling and leadership has been recognized by his peers, and his commitment to making a difference continues to guide his work.

Whether developing innovative solutions, mentoring emerging leaders or crafting designs that resonate, Caleb remains dedicated to creating meaningful impact.

In his personal life Caleb enjoys hiking, falconry, gliding, rebuilding Land Rovers and exploring the open road. He has a passion for collecting unique and well-crafted shoes, appreciating both their design and history. He cherishes time with family, friends and his three Jack Russell terriers, and finds inspiration in travel and the natural world.

To learn more, visit:
www.calebsummerfelt.com
www.facebook.com/calebsummerfelt.speaks
www.instagram.com/caleb.summerfelt.speaks
www.linkedin.com/in/calebsummerfelt
www.youtube.com/@calebsummerfelt

CHAPTER 3

LIVE BETTER, SERVE BETTER

By Dustin Kulling

"Show me a hero, and I'll write you a tragedy."
—F. SCOTT FITZGERALD

There comes a moment in every officer's career when you catch your reflection in a locker room mirror after a long, hellish shift and you wonder, "What the hell happened to me?"

It isn't one explosive incident that triggers that thought; often, it's the slow accumulation of countless shifts, the echo of blaring sirens, and the heavy silence that follows the chaos. Over time, wearing the badge has cost me far more than just my physical health—it has stripped away pieces of my soul and reshaped my mind, body, and spirit in ways I never imagined.

I remember the first day I put on the uniform. I was a wide-eyed rookie fueled by a desire to protect and a firm belief that my training would prepare me for any challenge. But nothing in the academy could have prepared me for the relentless physical and mental toll awaiting me in the field.

Nearly thirty years in the profession has taught me that we aren't just officers; we are tactical athletes. Every day, we are pushed to extremes that most people wouldn't even dare imagine. I've sprinted after suspects for blocks on end, my lungs burning, as every second counted between life and death. I've scaled fences, dashed up flights of stairs, and traversed narrow ledges where one misstep could cost me everything. Yet it wasn't just the physical strain that wore me down—my mind took a beating as well.

Luckily, I survived the extreme mental toll and I'm still here to tell this story. Many of my comrades weren't so lucky.

I spent nearly thirty years in law enforcement, many of which were spent patrolling some of California's toughest neighborhoods as a uniformed patrol deputy. Eight years I spent undercover at a task force with the DEA, FBI, ATF, and other state and local law enforcement agencies, dismantling large-scale drug trafficking organizations. I've served in command roles for over thirteen years. My experience as a crime fighter gave me a front-row seat to what many see only in movies. The stakes were always high, and our peak performance with communication, de-escalation, and negotiations was critical to success. On the streets it's always clear what's at stake: life itself.

My work as an undercover narcotics agent carried the same consequences. If I didn't carefully plan every aspect of my operation, Murphy's Law ensured the mission would go sideways and our undercover agents or informants could be killed. I've been punched, kicked, spit on, and ambushed by criminals, but my experience is not unique. That said, I would argue that most cops would rather face violence on the streets than be subjected to the office politics that pervade many law enforcement agencies. I've been subjected to what I would describe as some of the worst leadership imaginable. Although miserable at the time, I'm now thankful for it. Not only did it force me to hone my communication skills, but it showed me the kind of leader I wanted to be.

THE ART OF DE-ESCALATION

Throughout my career I worked for three sheriffs and five chiefs. Some were good; some were bad. I always respected the position, even if the man was a disaster. I was promoted to lieutenant in August of 2016 and reported to the captain of Field Forces, who, within a matter of months, shipped out to Quantico, Virginia, to attend the FBI National Academy. While he was gone, I was made acting captain. He gave me simple directions before he left: "Keep the ship headed the right way, Dustin." I appreciated this but found out it was easier said than done, especially in one of California's most beleaguered communities. I quickly went from supervising a small team to leading the entire Field Forces Division. This role gave me a seat at the decision-making table, but it also put me on the hook to deliver.

One morning I got a text from the sheriff's executive assistant: "He wants to see you. *Now.*" The night before, a prisoner had been released in error. Hours later he had stolen a car and assaulted someone, but my patrol team had caught and rebooked him before sunrise. The press, eager to paint us as reckless, had the story. I opened the conference room door to find the Custody Division captain looking shaken. Before I could sit, the sheriff stormed in, slammed a file onto the table, and shouted, "I want answers now!"

The Custody captain shrank into her seat. By then, I'd been practicing yoga for many years and had nearly mastered the art of staying calm in tense encounters. I'd taught hundreds of law enforcement students my Principles of De-escalation course, which incorporated breathing exercises and the science behind stress. It was time to see if those tools would be just as effective with my boss! I took a slow inhale, held my breath for a moment, then exhaled deliberately, feeling the tension settle. I paused to read between the lines and determined that the Custody captain needed support and the sheriff needed reassurance.

Calmly I explained that our team had recovered the suspect and rebooked him. The sheriff wasn't satisfied. "Why was he released in error?" I had no idea. That wasn't my division. But I knew what he really wanted—he needed to face the press with confidence to avoid looking incompetent. His anger was fueled by the pressure of public perception, not the mistake. I kept my voice even. "Sheriff, I know you need a solid response for the press. Catching the suspect isn't enough—we need to stop these mistakes for good. I don't know why it happened, but if you give me time, I'll work with Custody and get you answers."

Finally, he exhaled. "Get it done," he said before storming out.

The Custody captain, visibly shaking, finally met my eyes. I said, "Let's figure this out together." She nodded, relieved.

We fixed the problem, trained staff to prevent future errors, and gave the sheriff a solution to share with the press.

Lesson: De-escalation isn't about proving who's right. It's about understanding what's at stake for the other person. The sheriff needed credibility. The Custody captain needed support. By controlling my breathing and staying calm, I was able to read the room and de-escalate the situation. One of the best things you can do in a heated moment is refrain from adding to the chaos and instead pause, investigate, and lend your calm.

Find the Motivators

The first time I bought narcotics undercover, I learned the most important lesson in negotiation: Figure out what the other party wants, or risk being shot.

I was sitting in the driver's seat of my black Mustang, an informant twitching beside me. He was the only reason I was there—you don't just walk into a world like this. You need someone to introduce you. The problem? Informants are unreliable at best, addicts themselves at worst. This one had already gotten himself busted, and now he was flipping, giving up his dealer in exchange for leniency.

I had a wire strapped to my chest and a gun tucked into the small of my back. Two teams were in place: one monitoring from a van a few hundred yards away, the other, the react team, standing by in case things went south. "She'll be here in ten minutes," he muttered.

Suddenly a full-size black Tahoe parked in front of me, boxing me into the worst possible position. The passenger door opened, and the woman stepped out. But the real problem sat inside the Tahoe: three Hispanic males, two in the back wearing red. Gang members. And that's when my wire went dead.

Panic surged through me. I was cut off with no way to signal for help. Then the informant's breath hitched beside me. He recognized them—and he owed them money.

We needed to get out of there. I turned the key, but the Mustang didn't even click. Dead battery. No wire. No car. No backup. The woman approached the passenger side, and as she leaned in, I saw movement inside the Tahoe and assumed they were reaching for guns. I had two choices: get out and run, leaving the informant behind to die, or negotiate my way out.

She handed me the bag, but it was light. She was shorting me, and I told her so. She shrugged, saying, "The price just went up." That's when I saw it clearly: greed. That was the motivator. Not respect, not territory—money. I needed to control the narrative.

The doors of the Tahoe cracked open. I smiled and leaned in, using my best late-night radio-host voice. "I don't even know if this is any good. Let me test it out. If it's solid, I'll buy a pound. Thirty grand." They looked at each other, nodded and left. I exhaled, grabbed my phone, and made the call. Surveillance tailed them, and by the end of the operation, we had their weapons and multiple pounds of meth and made several arrests.

That day, my life depended on two main factors. The first was figuring out what was driving the criminals. Everyone has a motivator. Greed, fear, desperation—whatever it is, once you identify it, you can control the game. The second was managing my delivery. People don't just hear words; they react to tone and body language. A smile can disarm, a calm voice can defuse.

You don't win negotiations with force—you win them with understanding. Should you seek to have empathy even for a criminal? Absolutely, if you want to get out of there alive.

A PIVOT INTO NEW PURPOSE

Late in my career my mentor wanted to promote me. I resisted. I was living my dream. Undercover work meant a long beard, no uniform, and the thrill of being a narc. But he made me look around. "If you don't step up, these guys will be your boss."

So, I was promoted. First to sergeant in one of the busiest, most dangerous areas. Then I oversaw hostage negotiations and SWAT. I kept climbing—earned degrees, attended Command College, won awards, and within two years of making lieutenant, I became a captain.

When I reached the ceiling, I faced a choice: run for sheriff or take a new path. I pursued the latter, setting myself up to be the next chief of police in Coronado, a world away from Stockton. It was pristine, affluent—the opposite of everything I knew. I sacrificed friendships and stability to move there, only to watch the chief retire abruptly, a new city manager come in who wanted to clean house, and my promised future slip away. As acting chief I led through a devastating natural disaster and earned the support of the department but was ultimately passed over for someone with less experience. I was done.

I had left everything behind for this job, and now it was over. I was shocked and devastated. My wife and I moved to Florida to be close to our grandchildren, but as the weight of this loss pressed down on me, depression set in. This is an epidemic that no one talks about.

You see, years before, after just nine days on the job, I killed someone with my bare hands. Although I was exonerated, I never fully processed it. I see dead people all around me, faces whose last moments I had witnessed. And in the quiet hours, when there is no radio chatter or urgent call to answer, the cumulative weight of decades on the force becomes all too palpable. With too much time to think, the physical pain that once blurred into the background screamed for attention, and every unsolved case, every act of violence I had witnessed, made its way to the front of my mind. The silence became a gathering place for the ghosts of my past.

And I'm not alone. Many of my colleagues suffer from PTSD. Many are on their third or fourth marriage. Many are alcoholics. In 2019 more officers in the US committed suicide than were killed in the line of duty. I was struggling to fill the void and to make sense of it all when a mentor in San Diego called and told me about a statewide wellness initiative for 100,000 officers in California. They asked me to be part of it. I said yes. Now I work with the University of California San Diego, bridging the gap between law enforcement officers and mental-health programs, and helping others has been a massive help to *me*.

What I know now is that it's vital to reclaim a sense of self that goes beyond the uniform. I now see that the path to wellness is a deliberate, ongoing process—a daily commitment to caring for oneself so that we can continue to serve with clarity and compassion. In my work with the University of California San Diego I teach a program that proactively addresses six domains of wellness that will support peak performance and long-term survivability. Imagine a future where every officer feels truly supported—a future where mental health is treated throughout the career and not just at the end.

I'm working on my PhD, and this summer I'll start my dissertation. Through my research I seek to uncover the impact of connection and purpose as moderators of suicidal ideation in law enforcement officers. Now I'm taking this work further, speaking to agencies, working with chiefs across the country, and ensuring officers learn to protect not just their communities but themselves.

Law enforcement is about service, but in serving others, we often lose sight of ourselves. That's when we lose our compass. If we take care of ourselves first—physically, mentally, emotionally—we can better serve our communities, our families, and ourselves.

Tactical empathy is more than a tool for negotiations; it's a tool for life. As an undercover agent, I had to build instant rapport with drug traffickers. As a leader, I had to defuse conflict in high-stakes situations. But I've used the same principles to strengthen my marriage, understand my children, and even get a table at a packed restaurant on a Saturday night.

If you're facing an impossible conversation, the key is to empty your glass. Set aside your preconceptions, not to abandon them but to create space for understanding. Whether you're negotiating with a suspect, leading a team, or navigating personal relationships, tactical empathy is the bridge to resolution. It helps us win conversations, but more importantly, it helps us heal.

When you're backed into a corner, remember, you hold the pen. When the path seems fixed, that's your cue to flip the script—turn the chaos into clarity, the pain into purpose, and the challenges into a story worth telling, because if you can change the narrative, you can change—and possibly save—your own life.

About Dustin

Capt. Dustin Kulling (ret.) is a distinguished law enforcement professional with over twenty-nine years of experience dedicated to leadership, training, and officer wellness. A first-generation American on his father's side, Dustin's unwavering commitment to faith, family, and service has defined his career and shaped his approach to policing.

Dustin spent eight years working undercover in narcotics, investigating large-scale drug-trafficking organizations with international reach. Rising through the ranks, he oversaw over 250 sworn and professional staff and managed a budget exceeding fifty-eight million dollars. His leadership extended across diverse specialized units, including SWAT, Hostage Negotiations, Explosives Ordnance Disposal, Crime Analysis, Unmanned Aerial Systems, K9, Boating Safety, Communications, and Community Programs.

Dustin graduated from the prestigious California P.O.S.T. Command College, earning the coveted Hank Koehn Memorial Award. His fourteen-month research project examined the impact of technology on law enforcement force encounters. He has developed and delivered science-based coursework exploring the intersection of officer wellness, de-escalation, and tactical decision-making. As a recognized subject-matter expert, Dustin has shaped statewide training curricula, including California P.O.S.T.–certified courses in de-escalation and critical-incident tactics.

A passionate advocate for officer wellness, he is an instructor for Yoga for First Responders, teaching resilience techniques to first responders. Dustin has lectured extensively on best practices for agencies establishing comprehensive wellness programs and played a key role in developing initiatives that integrate peer support, chaplaincy, and mental-health resources to enhance officer performance and longevity. His expertise has shaped statewide policies, including internal-affairs and data-compliance regulations.

Academically, Dustin is pursuing a PhD in communication, researching law enforcement suicide prevention. His deep understanding of contemporary policing challenges has made him a sought-after instructor and presenter for wellness initiatives.

Dustin resides in Florida with his wife, Patricia, and they are celebrating over thirty-three years of marriage. They have three adult children: Joseph, a police officer and former US Navy service member; Rachael, a workers' compensation insurance professional; and Asher, a college student. They are also proud grandparents to Abigail, Ethan, and Anna.

Now, with decades of experience, Dustin is channeling his passion for officer wellness into writing, sharing vital insights to improve the well-being, resilience, and effectiveness of those who serve.

CHAPTER 4

FLIPPING THE SCRIPT FROM PAIN TO PURPOSE

By Ed Harris

I was eight years old the day my ten-year-old brother died in my arms.

We had just come home from church, and Ricky said his stomach hurt. The next morning, my mother told me she was going to let Ricky stay home from school and that I could too. I was happy, always eager to spend time with my older brother. But by midmorning, Ricky was still not up. When I walked into his room to wake him, he was purple.

I called his name. Nothing. My mom ran in, then shook him and called his name, but he was unresponsive. She sent me running next door for help. When I got back, Ricky was already being carried to the car. I sat in the back seat, cradling him for the twenty-five-minute ride to the hospital. Every bump in the road felt as though it might break him. My mom kept telling me to keep him awake.

So I talked to him. "You OK?" I whispered. "Yeah," he mumbled back. Then came the sound that still keeps me up some nights. He lurched forward and threw up blood all over the floorboard and then went completely still. And I knew. Even before we pulled up to the hospital, even before my dad ran out to carry him inside, even before the doctors worked on him for hours—I knew that somewhere on that drive, somewhere between my words and his silence, Ricky left.

They pronounced him dead a couple of days later. A routine surgery he had had a year before unleashed an infection in his body that he was unable to fight. When you lose your protector at

41

eight years old, something shifts inside you. Ricky wasn't just my brother. He was my shield. He was the fastest, strongest, smartest kid I knew, the one who made friends everywhere we went and stood between me and the bullies. He always, always looked out for me, and I could not fathom returning home without him.

In the years that followed, the grief didn't end. It didn't follow some clean, five-step process as they say it does. It carved itself into the shape of my life, fracturing the dynamic of our household and weaving its way into every milestone, every birthday, every big moment. There was always the same empty seat next to me, the same ache that whispered, "He should be here for this." But there was something else too. Even as a kid I felt this quiet, undeniable sense of purpose, like somehow I was supposed to carry forward the part of Ricky that didn't get the chance to grow up, the part of him that didn't get to make his mark. I didn't just want to live my life—I wanted to make up for the piece of the world we lost when we lost him. That hole has been with me for forty-two years, and it's the reason I do what I do. Today, I am the founder of Apogee Wealth Management, and my mission is to fight for the underdog.

It's why I show up for people who feel unseen. It's why I walk away from business deals that cross ethical lines, no matter the cost. It's why I built a firm where people aren't just accounts—they're families who've trusted us with their futures. Ricky protected me. Now I protect others. And what I've come to realize is that the deepest losses plant the deepest purpose. When you know what it feels like to lose someone who always looked out for you, it's only natural that your life centers on looking out for everyone else.

The Apogee Approach

The word *apogee* marks the highest, most exalted point—the peak of an orbit that is the farthest distance from the pull of the earth. It's that rare place where everything aligns, and momentum carries you as far as you were designed to go.

When I founded Apogee Wealth Management, that word wasn't

just a name; it was a promise, a promise that we wouldn't settle for average and that those who trust us with their life's savings would experience something higher, something better than just another financial transaction. For me, wealth management isn't really about money. It's about people. It's about the stories behind the numbers, the fears behind the spreadsheets, the dreams hidden inside those account balances. That's where empathy comes in. I used to think sales and negotiations were about winning and closing the deal, but the deeper I got into this work, the more I saw that real success—whether it's helping someone plan for retirement or navigating a high-stakes deal—comes from understanding people on a level most are too busy or too guarded to explore. Empathy, when practiced with intention, is not just something you turn on to be polite. It's the key that gets you beneath the surface of what people say and into the truth of what they mean.

When I sit down with a family, I'm not just listening to their goals. I'm listening for what's unspoken. I mirror their language. I name the emotions in the room. I pay attention to the pauses and the words they avoid, because the point of connection isn't to manipulate or maneuver—it's to understand. And when you truly understand someone, the whole game changes. Our goal is to use strategic communication to take people further than they thought they could go, and to create an experience where people feel safe, seen, and served at the absolute highest level. The real pinnacle of this work isn't just financial growth; it's human connection. The win isn't me over you; it's creating an outcome where no one has to lose—which, in essence, is the most exalted point, apogee.

But as you know, money is one of the most emotionally charged topics there is. That's why strategic communication isn't just helpful—it's essential.

THE DISCIPLINE OF STAYING FOCUSED

In any negotiation there's one rule that separates the professionals from the amateurs: Stay focused on the problem you're trying to solve. It sounds simple, but when the stakes are high, it becomes one of the hardest disciplines to hold.

I was working with a client who wanted part of his portfolio to be stable and protected from market volatility. That was the problem we were solving, plain and simple. But the moment I recommended a potential solution, the conversation drifted. He'd read negative headlines. Friends had warned him. He'd heard horror stories about high fees and false promises. Believe me, I have seen my own share of horror stories about products being used without the proper due diligence and care expected from a fiduciary like me. Suddenly we weren't talking about his portfolio anymore. We were lost in a debate about whether the tool is "good" or "bad." And that's the trap so many people fall into.

They start arguing about the tool instead of the task. They defend their position, their opinion, their pride, and forget why they sat down at the table in the first place. But negotiation isn't about defending your position; it's about solving the problem. So I brought the conversation back to that. I said, "You told me you want stability. If not this tool, then how do you suggest we create it?" And that's the key.

When you strip away the noise and focus on the goal, the conversation becomes productive again. You explore options, compare solutions, and get back to work solving the actual problem, not circling around distractions or letting fear drive the outcome.

This is where most negotiations go sideways.

People get stuck in defending or attacking an idea instead of collaborating on a solution. They let noise pull them off course and forget what winning even means. The win isn't proving you're right. The win is solving the problem better than anyone else could.

The product is just a product. What matters is whether the solution serves the need. This is why the best negotiators, the ones who consistently win, aren't the loudest or most aggressive; they're the ones who keep bringing the conversation back to center, back to the core objective at hand. When you stay focused on solving the problem, the path forward always becomes clear. And that clarity wins deals, builds trust, and creates lasting success.

SIT IN THE SEAT OF AUTHORITY

Most of us can remember having a teacher that everyone feared. They would stomp into the classroom, voice raised, fingers pointing, and do everything they could to let you know who was boss. I don't know about you, but while I may have feared that teacher, I never learned from them. Authority in a room isn't always about who called the meeting, who owns the title, or who's sitting at the head of the table. Real authority is claimed in quieter ways— through posture, presence, and the questions you choose to ask.

I learned this walking into what could have been a hostile meeting. I was sitting down with an executive team, and they weren't thrilled with me. I had already voiced serious concerns about the way business was being handled, and the tension was thick. It would have been easy to play defense, but instead, I made a deliberate choice to sit in the seat of quiet authority. I walked in with a simple notepad and pen. No grandstanding. No speeches. I took my seat, opened my notebook, and began asking questions, interview style.

And that changed everything. Questions are subtle power moves. They signal control without aggression, put the other side on the record, and shift the dynamic from you defending yourself to them having to *explain* themselves. I listened, wrote down their answers, and asked more questions. Slowly, as the conversation unfolded, the holes in their logic became impossible to ignore— not because I argued or raised my voice but because the right questions exposed the cracks. And as those cracks appeared, the power in the room quietly shifted.

You don't have to dominate to be in charge. You don't have to overpower anyone to lead the conversation. The person asking the questions is the one steering the ship. In negotiation, leadership and business, this is one of the most effective strategies there is: Lead the room without needing anyone to know you're leading it.

THE POWER OF KNOWING THEIR AUTOPILOT

Every person you meet operates with an internal setting—a psychological autopilot—that guides their decisions, whether they realize it or not. It's their default mode, the invisible script they follow, no matter how much logic you throw at them. And if you don't take the time to identify it, you'll waste energy trying to negotiate against something that isn't going to move. I worked with a client who on paper was in perfect shape. He had more money than he needed, no major legacy concerns, and every stress test we ran—market crashes, healthcare costs, Social Security failures—showed the same result: He was going to be fine. So when I pointed out that he didn't need to keep paying into an expensive longevity insurance policy, the math was obvious. It wasn't necessary. There was no risk of him running out of money. But here's where most people mess up. He wasn't making the decision based on math. This was psychological.

As we talked, he finally admitted, "I just like the idea of having it." Even though he didn't need it and the numbers didn't justify it, what he wanted was peace of mind. It made him feel better. Period. And for him, that feeling was worth the cost. It wasn't about markets or projections, so my data was meaningless to him. It was about his autopilot—the part of him that needed that safety net to feel comfortable enough to spend and enjoy his life. And here's the critical lesson: My job wasn't to fix his autopilot or argue him out of it. My job was to identify it, acknowledge it, accept it, and work *with* it. When you stop trying to change people and start understanding them, you create space for better decisions—ones that honor how they're wired while still moving the conversation forward. Sometimes the most effective thing you can do is name what's happening, respect it, and build the strategy around it.

When people feel understood, they stop resisting and defending, and from there real progress happens. So the next time you're sitting across from someone who just won't budge, ask yourself, "Am I fighting their logic, or their autopilot?" Once you know the difference, you'll stop wasting time trying to reprogram what was never yours to change—and build bridges instead of divides.

Fighting for the Underdog

Looking back, I can see how my life has been shaped by the people who believed in me when I didn't know how to believe in myself. When Ricky died, something in me shifted forever. I lost not just my brother but my protector—the one person who made sure I was safe, seen, and never left to fight alone. And from that moment on I carried this quiet promise that if I couldn't have him watching out for me anymore, then I would become that person for others.

That's the thread that's run through every part of my life, whether I recognized it at the time or not.

It's why I fight so hard for my clients and refuse to let people get taken advantage of. It's why I sit at tables where the odds are stacked and ask the hard questions until the truth reveals itself.

I know what it feels like to be the underdog. I also know what it feels like to have someone believe in you so deeply that you start believing in yourself again. For me, I had several mentors over the years who spoke purpose into me when I had none. They helped me see that my contribution mattered and that no matter how broken I felt, I still had something left to give. It was around my late teens that I stumbled on the book *Inside Out* by Dr. Larry Crabb—a book that flipped a switch in my teenage mind and taught me that change starts from within. I learned that I couldn't lead others until I learned to lead myself. At the end of the day my goal is to stand up for people who have worked hard and who need someone in their corner protecting them. I do it for the kid I used to be, for the brother I lost, and for the underdog who deserves to have someone on their side. Ultimately, the greatest purpose we can ever fulfill is to become for others what we once needed most.

And if you ask me, that's not just good business; it's the only kind of business worth being in.

About Ed

Ed Harris is the founder and CEO of Apogee Wealth Management, as well as the driving force behind Apogee Wealth Academy, a 501(c)(3) organization dedicated to helping individuals and families build brighter financial futures through education. With a passion for making financial concepts accessible, Ed empowers people to take control of their financial well-being, guiding them toward confidence and security in their financial decisions.

Ed's journey of service began at the young age of fifteen when he entered the ministry, instilling in him a deep sense of purpose and a desire to uplift others. This early experience shaped his values and commitment to helping those around him, a theme that resonates throughout his professional life. With over twenty years of experience in the financial sector, he combines professional expertise with a genuine commitment to serving his clients. Through Apogee Wealth Management, Ed helps clients navigate complex financial landscapes, ensuring they have the knowledge and strategies needed to achieve their long-term goals.

His holistic approach to wealth management focuses not only on investment strategies but also on the emotional and psychological aspects of financial decision-making. Ed understands that financial health is intertwined with personal values and life goals. By taking the time to listen to his clients and understand their unique situations and aspirations, he tailors his advice to meet their specific needs, fostering a sense of trust and partnership.

Alongside his wife, Melissa, Ed raises their five children with values rooted in health, fitness, and personal growth. Family is at the core of his life, and he believes in leading by example. Whether cheering on their kids at football, track, basketball, or gymnastics events, or fostering meaningful connections through his work, Ed brings warmth, care, and encouragement to everything he does. He actively participates in community events and workshops, sharing his knowledge to help others improve their financial literacy.

An advocate for financial literacy initiatives, Ed believes that education is the key to breaking the cycle of financial insecurity. Through Apogee Wealth Academy, he aims to reach underserved communities, providing resources and support to help individuals and families achieve financial independence. His vision is to create a world where everyone has the tools and knowledge to make informed financial decisions, ultimately leading to a more secure and prosperous future for all. Ed Harris is not just a financial adviser; he is a beacon of hope and a catalyst for change in the lives of many.

CHAPTER 5

SHATTERING SELF-LIMITING BELIEFS

The Key to Conquering the Silent Saboteur

By David Howell

The airplane idled in the darkness, the sky nothing but a pitch-black void. It had to be that way. Any light might alert the enemy to our presence. My heart raced as the door to the plane opened, and I suddenly had just seconds to calm my nerves, pray that my parachute opened, and do what I had gone there to do: *jump*.

They say the most dangerous enemy you'll ever face is the one you can't see, but in moments like that, it's not the darkness that can sabotage a mission. It's the voice of self-doubt.

I served eighteen years in the reserves, a paratrooper by choice. I signed up for the kind of insanity most people steer clear of—jumping out of perfectly good airplanes with nothing but a thin sheet of fabric and the hope it operates as it's supposed to. And when the moment comes, there is no time for hesitation. You jump, because that's what you're trained to do. Before you can engage with the battle on the ground, you've got to win the battle in your mind. You've got to quiet the inner saboteur who's whispering, "You're not ready. You're going to fail. You're not cut out for this."

In those operations, I relied on the TCUP method—thinking clearly under pressure. That's what separates those who make it from those who freeze. Either you learn to control fear, or it controls you, because when it's time to jump, there's no room for panic. You have to trust your training, trust your team, trust your equipment, and, most of all, trust yourself.

It's not about the jump. It's about the *belief* you've built leading up to that moment when the plane door opens. The hours of training, the reps, the drills—each one designed to beat back that inner saboteur screaming at you to quit. I've faced that same voice of self-doubt every time the stakes got high, whether it was mid-mission, making the tough choice to leave combat to be with my family, or risking everything to build my own business. What I know now is that in high-stakes moments, you don't negotiate with your inner critic. You silence it. You lean on your training, your faith, your preparation. And you jump.

The truth is simple: *The inner critic wins only if you let it.* And I don't negotiate with terrorists—not even the one in my own head.

GO AHEAD, LOSE YOUR MIND!

I come from humble beginnings—a working-class mining village in Yorkshire. As a rugby player and one of three brothers, I learned early that your word was your bond, and how you carried yourself mattered—on and off the field.

From the time I was twelve or thirteen, I was always curious about human behavior. Rugby became my first real teacher of it. I was captain of the team, then played for the county, then was selected for the under-twenty-one for England. You learn fast that leadership isn't about shouting loudest but about how you show up when it matters most—on the pitch and off it.

My parents must have seen something in me early because when I was thirteen, they gave me Rudyard Kipling's poem "If—." I didn't know then how much those words would shape me, especially the line etched above the players' entrance at Wimbledon's Centre Court: "If you can meet with Triumph and Disaster and treat those two impostors just the same..." That line became a reminder that the highs and lows are both illusions—and neither defines you. I didn't choose to go into financial services; it chose me. I was recruited into finance and did well enough that eventually I decided to start my own business.

That's where the real fight started—not outside but within. The voice in my head—the same one that whispered before every jump—started screaming: "You're not ready. You're not good enough. Who the hell do you think you are?" The weight of impostor syndrome pressed down hard. And then, somewhere in that fog, I remembered Kipling's words again: "If you can trust yourself when all men doubt you, but make allowance for their doubting too..." If I could trust myself to jump out of a plane, surely I could be trusted to jump *into* leadership.

The reality is that the amygdala in our brains hasn't evolved much in twenty-five hundred years. Fight, flight or freeze still reigns. That monkey mind is hardwired to scream, "Danger," even when the only threat is to our ego. It's not wrong; it's just doing its job. The trick is learning to coach yourself through it. I had to learn to be my own coach first—to sit with fear, acknowledge it, even thank it: "I hear you. Thank you for trying to protect me." And then step forward anyway. That's what leadership is—understanding that your greatest opponent isn't out there. It's the silent saboteur inside. But once you recognize it, once you reframe the narrative, you unlock the ability to lead yourself. We have to be able to observe our minds through an objective lens. Imagine a fish leaping out of water and catching its own reflection. We can learn to see ourselves not as our minds but as the observer of them. That's where the power is.

My business grew from a fledgling idea to a global enterprise with clients across the Middle East, Europe, Asia, and beyond. It didn't happen because I was the smartest guy in the room but because I won the only negotiation that ever really matters: the one within.

This quote, widely attributed to Wallace Wattles, says it best: "Success is not the result of hard work, but of right thinking."[1] That's the secret. You think your way into confidence. You silence the inner saboteur—and you *jump*.

FLIPPING THE INNER SCRIPT

Have you ever found yourself in a moment when the toughest negotiation wasn't with a client or a competitor but with your own ruthless inner voice? That inner critic is an expert at spinning tall tales and worst-case scenarios, but here's the truth: Doubt is a thought—not a fact. Not every thought deserves a seat at your table, and there are steps you can take to keep uninvited guests away!

The first step is to acknowledge the doubt, but don't identify with it. It's there, but it's not *you*. It's noise. Observe it for what it is—an illusion. Smoke and mirrors created by your own mind. I used to believe I wasn't capable of leading a thriving business, guiding clients with absolute confidence, or making decisions that impacted people's lives. I told myself those stories until they felt real. But the moment I stopped entertaining my own self-imposed limits, everything shifted. My capability was there—buried under layers of doubt—just waiting to be recognized. I used a framework for when the noise gets too loud and the fear feels real. I call it The GAME Plan—because success, like any goal or negotiation, needs a plan.

G—Goals
A—Actions
M—Means (your talents, your network, your resources)
E—Execution

This is how you silence the inner critic. You give your mind a mission and a road map. Without a map to follow, the brain defaults to fear. A solid blueprint is your weapon against your default monkey brain! The next step? Challenge your inner critic head-on. Most people fixate on the worst-case scenario, but the better strategy is to ask yourself, "What if I succeed?"

I'll never forget the first time I was offered the chance to speak in front of a roomful of influential leaders. My gut reaction wasn't excitement. It was pure fear. What if I stumble over my words?

What if they laugh? What if they realize I don't belong there?" FEAR: false evidence appearing real.

That's when I flipped the script. I asked myself, "What if this moment defines the next chapter of my journey? What if this opens the door to everything I've been working for?"

I leaned in to fear and accepted it as part of the process. When I stepped on that stage, I didn't just prove something to the audience; I proved something to myself. Fear didn't own me—and I very much belonged there. Now, here's the tough part: This isn't something you do once. Fear is like a phoenix, always rising from the ashes at the worst times.

When my business really took off, you would think my confidence would soar, but that's not what happened. I suddenly had clients in Europe, the Middle East, and the Far East. I was leading initiatives and managing jurisdictions I'd never imagined. And the voice came roaring back: "Am I really capable of leading a company at this level?" I immediately recognized the voice of my inner critic and did what I now teach others. I sat down, grabbed a pen, and wrote down every win, every time I'd faced fear and come out on the other side. The deals closed. The clients served. The people who believed in me. Seeing it on paper shattered the illusion.

The butterflies? They never go away. The trick is to get those butterflies flying in formation and in the direction you need them to go. That's The GAME Plan. That's how you beat the inner saboteur. And that's how you win the only negotiation that really matters—the one within.

SHIFT YOUR FOCUS

One of the fastest ways to silence your inner critic is to shift your focus outward, to stop obsessing over yourself and start serving others. That's where confidence lives—in empathy, connection, and the authentic desire to help and understand others.

I learned that lesson in the Middle East, where the rules of the game are different and the stakes are high. You don't walk into a room and start talking about contracts and numbers. If you do, you lose before you even sit down.

In that culture, business is personal. The negotiations don't begin in a boardroom but around a fire in the middle of the desert, sharing coffee and a smoke.

That's when it hit me: *This* was the real negotiation. I couldn't lead with the deal; I had to build the relationship. I had to build trust. The best strategy here was to have no strategy at all, but rather just be present, authentic, and genuinely interested in getting to know the men across from me.

What I learned out there sitting cross-legged in the sand, passing that pipe, was that authenticity is the bridge to connection, to leadership, and, most importantly, to confidence.

Confidence isn't about being the loudest voice in the room or knowing all the answers. It's about being anchored in who you are and the values you hold. It's about slowing the conversation down and building a bridge that's strong enough to support a deeper discussion. Something powerful happens when you operate that way. When you aim to serve and to make the other person feel seen and heard, you stop performing and start belonging. You flip the script from self-doubt to self-trust. And the inner critic? It has no power here.

Authenticity creates empathy. Empathy creates confidence. And confidence kills the inner critic.

Every time.

SILENCE THE INNER CRITIC

One of the most defining moments of my life wasn't building the business—it was deciding to let it go. Selling something I'd built from the ground up, brick by brick, deal by deal, was the ultimate negotiation, not just of contracts and numbers but of emotion, identity, and ego.

The toughest part was navigating the emotional connection to my business and to the people who helped power it. Some of my employees had become like family. I had no idea how they would feel and no clue what I would do next. Signing on that dotted line felt like stepping off a cliff. I'd built something that mattered, and walking away triggered every doubt I'd ever had as my inner saboteur started chirping, "Did I just make the biggest mistake of my life? Did I let people down?"

Ultimately, it all worked out and letting go wasn't failure; it was growth. It was making space for what was next. I'd given everything to that business, including time that could have been spent with my family on birthdays, anniversaries, and holidays I missed. Selling wasn't quitting. It was *choosing*—choosing my life, my family, my future.

The deal closed just before COVID hit. I sat down, poured myself a good drink, took a long breath, and felt something I hadn't felt in years—relief—not because I was free of the business but because I was free to ask the bigger question: What's next? What does the world need? What am I really here for? And the answer unfolded before me. Mastering my inner dialogue wasn't just something that shaped my career; it transformed my life. It made me resilient, intentional, and far less concerned with proving myself to anyone, especially that voice in my head. I learned to stop reacting to fear and start questioning it. I stopped seeking approval and started trusting my own judgment. That shift did more than build a business. It strengthened my relationships, deepened my conversations, and gave me the confidence to walk into any room, fully present, with nothing to prove.

Today, I am a consultant for a family office focused not just on wealth but well-being, and it's incredibly fulfilling to help a company whose values match my own. Every day, I get to tap into my areas of expertise and help my clients move toward their highest goals and dreams. It truly is an expression of my purpose, and you know what they say: Money might help you sleep, but purpose gets you out of bed!

The real wins are not about closing the deals. They're about conquering the one negotiation that defines us all: the one against our own self-doubt. That's where freedom lives—not in the absence of fear but in the mastery of it. When you learn to silence the inner critic, trust your own voice, and lead with conviction, fear may show up, but this time you'll be armed with a GAME plan.

And fear won't stand a chance.

> "Mastering others is strength. Mastering yourself is true power."[2]
>
> —LAO TZU

ENDNOTES

1. In *The Science of Getting Rich* (n.p., 2021), Wallace D. Wattles emphasizes the power of thought over mere effort, stating: "Do all the work you can do, every day, and do each piece of work in a perfectly successful manner; put the power of success, and the purpose to get rich, into everything that you do," Goodreads, accessed May 22, 2025, https://www.goodreads.com/author/quotes/65913.Wallace_D_Wattles?utm_source=chatgpt.com.

2. "Lao Tzu Quotes," BrainyQuote, accessed May 1, 2025, https://www.brainyquote.com/quotes/lao_tzu_130742.

About David

David is a highly respected financial-industry professional and business mentor, bringing over thirty-eight years of experience in financial planning and wealth management. A seasoned CEO and number one best-selling author, David is recognized as a thought leader in the field and is featured on *Hollywood Live*, as seen on ABC, NBC, CBS, and FOX, where he has shared expert insights on financial well-being.

Renowned for his ability to simplify complex financial concepts, David is a trusted voice not only for clients but also for professionals across the global financial community. His leadership and vision have helped shape the future of financial planning and continue to inspire the next generation of advisers.

Beyond his professional accomplishments, David is deeply committed to giving back. He has served as a magistrate, contributed to numerous charitable causes, and served in the Territorial Army. Outside of work he enjoys family life, traveling, and long walks with his dogs.

Connect with David:
david@drhowell.com
thegameplan.com

CHAPTER 6

TAMING ELEPHANTS AND CHAOS

By Robert Mason

"**J**ust tell us, is our daughter going to die?"

It's the kind of question you never imagine yourself asking, until the moment you do. Once it's out there, you realize just how quickly life can split into a before and after.

Before December 28, 2007, my world was exactly as it should be. My wife, Jana, and I had just welcomed our baby, Rebecca—a perfectly healthy and beautiful baby girl. She was our second child, our first daughter. The moment felt complete, like the start of something beautiful. And then, in an instant, it wasn't.

One minute I was preparing to buckle her into a car seat, ready to bring her home. The next, I was watching a team of nurses race down the hallway, my daughter cradled in their arms as they worked desperately to get her breathing again. They saved her, but a few minutes later she stopped breathing again. Twice in a matter of minutes I watched them pull her back from the edge. From the hallway to the neonatal intensive care unit (NICU), I kept replaying the same promise my wife insisted I make to her years earlier when preparing for the birth of our son Erik: "If they ever take our baby, you go with our baby. No matter what."

So I went. I stood by our daughter's side in that chaotic, whirring room of machines and wires, watching strangers fight for her life while I stood completely powerless. When it became clear they needed to move her to Toronto's Sick Kids Hospital, we knew things were serious, but nothing prepared me for the moment they closed the ambulance doors and said there wasn't room for us to ride with her. I watched as they drove away with my daughter, her life hanging in the balance, while my wife and I followed behind in stunned silence.

That hour-long drive was the longest of our lives.

Our baby girl Rebecca is seventeen now. She's healthy and thriving, and not a day goes by without awareness of just how lucky we are. Looking back, I see that experience for what it really was. Yes, it was trauma. Yes, it was fear unlike anything I'd ever known. But it was also the moment I learned the single most valuable skill I've carried into every part of my life since: how to show up and fight for what matters when you're not holding the right cards. What I realized in that moment and in the weeks that followed was although I could not save my daughter's life, I needed to build trust with those who could. I could stay calm. I could listen. I could ask the right questions. I could be a source of support for the folks looking for a solution. And today, that's exactly the work I do.

After nearly three decades in global supply chain leadership—from aerospace to consumer goods, overseeing everything from the technology in the Mars Rover to the orange juice in your fridge—I've learned the stakes are always high somewhere. Supply chain used to live quietly in the shadows. Then COVID hit, and suddenly the whole world understood what happens when systems break and people panic. Now I help organizations steady the chaos. I help leaders navigate high-stakes decisions with clarity and empathy. I teach teams how to communicate when everything is on the line.

And what I know is this: The same skills that kept me grounded at my daughter's bedside are the ones that keep companies afloat today. The stakes are different. The pressure may feel different. But the need for clear, calm, human connection is the same.

JUMP ON THE ELEPHANT

If you know there's an elephant in the room, there's a good chance everyone else sees it too. And until you address it, no one is hearing a word you say.

Jump on the elephant!

The clearest example of this in my life came within twenty-four hours of arriving at Toronto Sick Kids. My wife and I found ourselves in a small room with a doctor, a nurse, and—for the first time—a minister. That's when the elephant walked in alongside them.

The doctor started going over Rebecca's test results, taking the long way around the thing we couldn't ignore. The words didn't land. They couldn't, because until we knew whether our daughter was going to live or die, nothing else mattered. So, we stopped her. "Doctor, before we go any further, is she going to live?" "Oh—yes," she said, almost surprised by the question, "Yes, she's going to live." Just like that, the weight in the room shifted. Our minds cleared. Our bodies unclenched, and for the first time, we could actually hear what she was trying to tell us. That moment has never left me.

In work, just as in life, there's often an elephant. Maybe it's a missed deadline or a failed system. Maybe it's the unspoken fear that a project's off the rails or that someone's not up for the task. Whatever it is—if you don't name it, it owns the conversation. No one is fully present or fully listening. So, I say it. "Let's start by naming the elephant in the room."

Sometimes I get it exactly right. The other side breathes a sigh of relief because I've said what they couldn't, and we can finally move forward. But not always. I've called out what I *thought* was the elephant, but it turned out, it wasn't.

I once worked with a client whose planning system had a major flaw—a breakdown that I assumed was the big problem. It was costing them efficiency, eating up resources, and limiting how they operated. The fix would be expensive. So I called it out. They said, "That's not going to be a problem. We've got the resources." For me, it was the elephant. For them? Barely a blip on the radar. That taught me a great lesson. Calling out the elephant isn't just about clearing the air, it's about checking your assumptions, aligning realities, and making sure you're not fighting a battle no one else sees or cares about. Before your next high-stakes conversation, ask yourself, "What's the unspoken fear in the room? What's the question no one is asking? What's distracting everyone from hearing what actually matters?" Then lead with it. Name it. And watch how fast people start to actually listen. Because no real progress happens until the elephant is outed.

READ THE ROOM

In the chaos of the NICU, I knew I had a choice. I could be an emotional wreck sobbing in the corner, or the overbearing parent barking demands, shoving my way into every conversation. Or I could become a part of the solution. My wife and I couldn't control what was happening to our daughter, but we *could* control how we showed up for the people taking care of her. In that high-stakes environment, you quickly realize something: emotions are running the show. The doctors, the nurses, the specialists—they're all human. They're carrying the weight of life-or-death decisions every single day and if you don't acknowledge that reality, you're missing the opportunity to build the kind of trust that can change everything. That's where labeling became my greatest tool.

Labeling is simple but powerful. It's noticing what someone else is feeling and saying it out loud. Not to fix it or solve it, just to acknowledge it. And in those days sitting beside my daughter's incubator, I started using labels to build connections with the people who were responsible for my daughter's life. To a nurse wiping tears after a hard loss I would say, "It looks like today's been incredibly heavy." To a doctor who looked exhausted after a long shift I would say, "It looks like it's been a nonstop day." Every time I did, they opened up. They shared the story behind the expression. They filled in the gaps I couldn't see. In that process, rapport was born.

Why does that matter? Because in a place like the NICU—or any high-stakes situation—trust isn't optional. It's everything. Labeling created a connection. It told the people caring for our daughter, "We see you. We understand what this is costing you." What I learned is that labeling doesn't just help *them*, it helps *you*. When people feel seen, they share more information. It's a skill that can be ported into any negotiation. Labeling is putting words to someone else's emotions in a way that shows you're paying attention.

Could we have received the same excellent care from those doctors and nurses without these tools? Maybe. But I wasn't willing to take that risk. It wasn't manipulative. It was a genuine understanding that we were all in it together. What I know with certainty: When you're dealing with people—whether it's in a NICU, a boardroom, or a negotiation—strong relationships drive better outcomes.

The Magic of Mirroring

If labeling is the way to show people you *see* them, then mirroring is how you show people you're *with* them. If you've ever sat with a loved one in the hospital, you know facetime with the doctor is hard to come by. Doctors are rushed, overwhelmed, and quickly moving in and out on their rounds while juggling critical decisions. While always professional and informative, I could feel a wall between us. I needed to understand what was happening with my child and for that, I needed more of their time. Mirroring is the practice of repeating the last three to four words someone says, with a curious tone that invites them to keep talking. So, when a doctor explained Rebecca's latest numbers and said, "We're watching for signs of respiratory fatigue," I'd reflect it back—"Respiratory fatigue?" And then, just like that, they'd keep going. More detail. More insight. And here's the key—I wasn't always following every technical term they dropped. A lot of it was far beyond what I could process in real time. But mirroring kept the conversation alive. It brought us more information, more clarity, and most importantly, more comfort. Mirroring opened a dialogue.

The more I mirrored, the deeper they went. The deeper they went, the more comfortable they became. And the more comfortable they became, the stronger our relationship grew. When the next big decision came, we weren't just two worried parents sitting silently in the corner. We were part of the conversation. We were informed and engaged. In his book *If I Understood You, Would I Have This Look on My Face?* Alan Alda wrote, "Ignorance was my ally as long as it was backed up by curiosity. Ignorance without curiosity is not so good, but with curiosity it was the clear water through which I could see the coins at the bottom of the fountain." That's the beauty of mirroring. It taps into something universal: People want to feel heard and understood. Repeat the last three or four words they said, say them slowly and then let the other person pick it back up.

When people hear their own words reflected back to them, it levels the playing field, which makes them want to continue talking. The more they talk, the more you learn. And in any conversation, information is advantage.

LEAVE THE TABLE BETTER

If you've ever found yourself in a tense, high-stakes moment, you know the best outcomes are rarely born out of who talks the loudest. They come from who listens the hardest.

I saw this in the NICU, I see it at home, and I encounter it every day with my business.

As a consultant, I spend my time helping businesses untangle complex problems, guiding leaders through moments where the pressure is high, and the stakes are real. The same skills I first sharpened at my daughter's bedside are the ones I rely on now to get the best deals for my clients.

I had a mentor at Coca-Cola named Rob Haddock who showed

me what real leadership looked like. Rob could keep his head when everyone else was losing theirs, and somehow, without anyone realizing it, guide a room full of strong personalities straight toward his vision.

Rob taught me how to work at both the tactical and strategic level at the same time—handling the day-to-day details without losing sight of the bigger picture. That's how we create real change: knowing when to zoom in and fix what's broken, and when to zoom out and make sure we're still heading in the right direction. He taught me when to take the reins and when to be flexible and flow with the current. That balance has been critical, not just in my career, but in my life. Because Rebecca's story didn't end with those terrifying first days in the NICU.

At eleven years old, the seizures began. They came fast. They came hard. They came despite every medication we tried. And just like before, we had to gather information. Stay calm. Build trust with the people searching for the answers. On November 28, 2024, Rebecca underwent neurosurgery at Toronto Sick Kids to control the seizures. Seizures that were emanating from the same area of the brain that caused her issues at birth. Once again, we found ourselves sitting in waiting rooms, asking questions, listening closely, mirroring back the words of the experts we trusted, labeling the fear in the room so we could clear it out and focus on what mattered.

Rebecca has been seizure-free since November. She is brilliant, flourishing, and a budding artist with a mind as creative as it is resilient. We're not all the way through it. We've got another six to eight months before we breathe all the way out. But every day, we get a little closer. And every day, I find myself going back to the same mantra that's guided me through all of it: Make it work. Make it better. Make it best. Never let it rest. Whether it's in a NICU, a boardroom, or across the dinner table, that's what negotiation really is. It's iteration. It's adjustment. It's staying curious. Staying engaged. Listening harder. Asking smarter questions. Getting just a little better with every single conversation. And if you take nothing else from this chapter, take this: You don't have to be the loudest voice in the room or have all the answers. Whether you're fighting for your child's life or closing the biggest deal of your career, the real win is when everybody leaves the table better than when they arrived.

As I reflect back, I realize how much my daughter has taught me. Rebecca has taught me the power of resilience. She has taught me the importance of deep connections. And from the second she was born, she taught me how to show up, how to fight for what mattered, and ultimately how to flip the script.

About Robert

Robert A. Mason is a renowned supply-chain executive and strategic leader with nearly three decades of experience spanning food and beverage, electronics manufacturing, and consumer packaged goods. As the founder of Mason Supply Chain Solutions, he has helped organizations streamline enterprise resource planning (ERP) systems, optimize operational efficiencies, and drive sustainable, bottom-line growth.

Throughout his career Robert has been instrumental in transforming supply-chain infrastructures, implementing cost-saving strategies, and generating multimillion-dollar efficiency improvements. His tenure at The Coca-Cola Co. and Celestica established him as an expert in optimizing supply-chain costs. Focusing on supply planning, demand planning, warehousing, and distribution, in conjunction with ERP optimization, he consistently delivers long-term, measurable business impacts.

A lifelong learner and executive strategist, Robert has refined his leadership expertise through Harvard Business School's Leadership Excellence Accelerated Performance (LEAP 2.0) program and advanced negotiation training with Chris Voss' Black Swan Group. Recognized for his strategic foresight, operational excellence, and ability to develop high-performing teams, he excels at driving business transformation, enhancing supply chain resilience, and fostering executive partnerships.

Beyond his professional achievements, Robert is an adventurer at heart, embracing a life of exploration and discovery. Based in Oshawa, Ontario, he enjoys traveling, camping, and boating with his wife, Jana, and their two children, Erik and Rebecca. A dedicated rucker, golfer, and lifelong hockey and lacrosse enthusiast, he is equally passionate about cooking, barbecue, and discovering new culinary experiences.

Robert lives by the philosophy "Make it work. Make it better. Make it best. Never let it rest."

For more insights, visit Mason Supply Chain Solutions:

www.masonsupplychain.com
mscs@masonsupplychain.com

CHAPTER 7

THE OPPORTUNITY TO FAIL

By Cal Hutson

"**T**he state of Missouri no longer requires your service," said the captain as he terminated my employment. I couldn't believe what I was hearing. My entire life plan shattered in a single sentence. As I made the two-hour drive from Jefferson City back to my home in Kansas City, the reality of what happened pressed on me with the weight of a thousand bricks. My dream—to serve and protect as a state trooper—had driven me relentlessly for years. Every mental test, every grueling physical exam, every nerve-wracking interview and polygraph was a step toward a destiny I'd envisioned since childhood.

On my twenty-fifth birthday, as I donned my uniform for the first time as a cadet in the Missouri State Highway Patrol, I believed I had finally achieved everything I'd worked for and thought my future was set.

Then, just one month in, they fired me. A single test—the requirement to name the county seat for every county—became my downfall. I aced eleven out of twelve names but couldn't remember the final name. When they posted the list of who passed and who needed to retake it, my name was not on the retake list. I knew I had failed it, but an oversight on their part had pushed me through, and I stayed quiet. When they finally realized their mistake, they saw my silence as an unforgivable act of dishonesty.

Now, as a forty-six-year-old business owner, I see that painful experience in a different light. That setback, as much as it broke me at the time, forged the foundation of the unexpected leadership journey I was about to take. It was a tough lesson—one that completely reshaped my understanding of effort, honesty, and the true essence of success.

Plot Twist

The day my dream crumbled, I had no road map. To make ends meet, I became a substitute teacher, a job I never imagined loving but one that gave me a chance to prove I had value. Yes, I did it for money, but I also needed to prove to myself after such a blow, integrity and reliability were still in me. It was in the classroom that I began to rebuild myself. Then life took another turn. My wife, a sign language interpreter, had an idea. She suggested that with my background in English and journalism I should train on a new software program. It wasn't something I had planned, but I gave it a shot. I hit a great streak. The work came in consistently, assignments piled up, and suddenly, the idea clicked. I could train others and assign these tasks, essentially building a business that offered robust transcription services. I took the leap and launched Quality Transcription Specialists, and before long I had clients across the entire country. It was a success I couldn't possibly have anticipated. Fifteen years later, with QTS still going strong, we opened BeeHive Homes of Grain Valley as franchisees. BeeHive Homes is a leader in assisted living and memory-care services across the United States. More than being an entrepreneur, I have valued the idea of reinvention. We don't have to be one thing forever.

Through these experiences, I've developed communication strategies that have contributed greatly to my growth. The entrepreneurial journey goes beyond business knowledge; it challenges endurance, skill, and empathy. Both the tough lessons and hard-won victories equipped me with strategies that shifted the odds in my favor, ultimately leading to success in both personal and professional aspects.

Keeping a Cool Head: A Lesson in Tactical Empathy

On his podcast Adam Carolla talked about gravity: If we don't move, our muscles atrophy. But when we engage with gravity—essentially choosing to embrace resistance—it makes us stronger. Life works the same way. The struggle, the friction—all of it's necessary to build resilience. We must learn to charge into the challenge, and one tool we need to bring with us is *empathy*.

I learned this in a high-stakes moment when I was co-owner of a sign language interpreting agency. My main role was to handle overdue payments. Often it was just an oversight, but in this case a client simply decided they weren't going to pay their bill. They owed us nearly $15,000 over a six-month period. My initial reaction was anger, but I had recently read *Never Split the Difference* by Chris Voss, so I knew I had to transition my anger into curiosity. It felt unnatural. I'd been raised by a mother who was loving but also a bit of a steamroller—might equaled right. That approach had shaped me, but it wasn't serving me anymore. I needed a better way. If I had approached this situation with force, I would have met equal resistance. Instead, I chose empathy. Not submission mind you, but strategic empathy. I asked myself, "How does this make sense to them?" The answer was simple. They saw no value in our work. Demanding, "Give us our $15,000!" wouldn't get me anywhere. I knew to have a favorable outcome, this couldn't be a gunfight; it had to be a chess match.

After some patient back-and-forth, the issue made it all the way to their CEO. He passed the buck immediately, saying an insurance company was responsible for payment, not them. He claimed his company had no obligation to pay for sign language interpreting services. I could have touted all the experience I had. Twenty years' worth, in fact. I could have schooled him on the ADA and equal-access laws, but that would've been pointless. His ego wasn't going to bow to my expertise. So instead, I dumped *my* ego and played to *his*. I wrote, "Wow! I didn't expect this to make it to the CEO, but I'm glad we have your support. I can imagine the surprise when you saw a bill for that amount of money, especially since this wasn't on your radar. Going forward, under what circumstances would your company pay for a sign language interpreter for a patient needing treatment?"

That one question changed everything. He responded, in writing, that if the insurance company wouldn't cover interpreting services, then the patient would have to pay. He also admitted that his company wasn't "set up to provide charity care." What he didn't realize was that he had just admitted, in writing, to discrimination. If this went to court, it would've cost his organization far more than $15,000.

My words appealed to his ego, and he let his guard down. Once the door was open, we walked right through it. In the end they paid 90 percent of what they owed us. They needed a small win, and we needed most of our money.

That experience proved something: If my younger, steamrolling-self had handled this, I would have blown the lid off in my first email and my company would have been out nearly $15,000. Being measured, patient, and methodical got us what we needed.

Here's the catch: Most people expect a fight, and that's why keeping a cool head is a powerful strategy. Most people don't expect true empathy and understanding from the other side. They come in on the defensive. Their amygdala gets fired up, and they brace for battle. When they're met with empathy, it disarms them, and suddenly you're no longer the enemy.

THE OPPORTUNITY TO FAIL: WINNING THE CONVERSATION THROUGH ACCOUNTABILITY

Smart business owners see failure as a way to get better. But the best business owners truly see it as an opportunity. When I screw up, I get excited because now I get to truly test my ability. I get the chance to fix it, sure, but I also get to show the person across the table what I'm made of and how I handle situations when they go south.

In the personal care home industry, when a resident gets out, it's called an elopement. The best-case scenario is that someone finds them quickly and brings them back safely. The state knows this happens occasionally, but families are often less understanding. In the first couple of months of being open, we had a near elopement happen. It was a shame because we had many of the necessary safety measures in our plan, but we were going through an extensive remodel. We were so new that the type of locks needed had not yet been installed. A resident's daughter was out of town when her mother got out. She was safe and just in the yard, but it was still a security glitch. The daughter was gracious, but I could sense she was boiling inside.

I took the *Never Split the Difference* approach. I didn't try to soften or minimize it. When she came into my office, I said, "We let you down. You trusted us with your mom, and she got out. There's no excuse for that." I could see it in her eyes: "That's right." In that moment, she relaxed a little because we were being culpable. Then I did something she wasn't expecting—I acknowledged how well she was handling it. "You have every right to tear me apart, but you're handling this with such grace, and I sincerely appreciate it. We can't change what happened, but we won't let this happen again." And we didn't.

From there we called the company installing the locks and expedited the process. We fixed the problem. More importantly, we worked the problem instead of letting the problem work *us*. This could have been a lawsuit. Instead, we turned it into a moment of trust building. The resident never actually left the property, but that didn't matter. What mattered was how we handled the failure.

Jocko Willink says in *Extreme Ownership*, "Leaders must own everything in their world." That's how we handled it. Clients give you opportunities to fail every day. What matters isn't the failure itself; it's how you respond. Do you make excuses? Or do you own it? Owning it defuses conflict and establishes trust. It might sound counterintuitive. Why would someone trust you if you failed? They don't trust you *because* you failed, but *despite* it. They trust you because you didn't insult their intelligence by lying or passing the buck.

Failing isn't the enemy, but failing without correction is lunacy. When you fail and own it, you show people what you're really made of—honesty, integrity and a willingness to lead.

THE HIDDEN KEY TO NEGOTIATION

In every negotiation there is a hidden piece of critical information—the *Black Swan*. The Black Swan, once discovered, can be the difference between success and failure. Placing your loved one in a care home is an emotional decision filled with doubt, guilt, and reluctance. Three weeks ago a family told us their father Dave needed care, and if nothing looked glaringly wrong when they visited, they wanted to reserve a room. It sounded urgent, so I assumed it was a slam dunk.

On the tour Dave was quiet. They assumed he'd want the larger suite, but when we stepped inside, his response was an instant, "No!" His daughter reminded him that he needed more care than his mother could provide and there was no alternative. His response? "Death!" And he meant it. This certainly wasn't going as planned. I had *their* support, but not *his*. Without his buy-in, the deal was dead in the water. This guy wasn't just hesitant. He had just told us he would rather die than move into our home. Talk about an uphill climb. There was a Black Swan there, and I needed to find it.

In my best late-night FM DJ voice, I said, "Dave, it seems like you're having reservations. What's going on?" He nodded toward the front and spoke one word: "Them." The residents. Upon arriving, he had seen some of our memory care residents, people with advanced dementia and Alzheimer's, being led around the room. It clicked.

"Oh, you feel like you don't belong here with *those people*, right?" He nodded. That was the Black Swan. Now I could work with it. I suggested his family go and speak to the other residents so they could ask questions. While they were doing that, I decided to treat Dave as the man he still was inside.

He loved Camaros; I love Camaros. He was a fan of KISS, so I talked about Gene Simmons' business ventures. It wasn't fake. It was a genuine desire to learn about the human across from me. By the time his family returned, he'd changed his mind. Finding the Black Swan isn't just about listening; it's about reading between the lines, speaking their language, and meeting them where they are. That's how bonds are built, trust is established, and deals are won. In this case, in forty-five minutes we went from "I'd rather die than live here," to, "Here's a check; I'm moving in."

THE BENEFIT OF BEING HUMAN

So many people say they are bad with faces and names, but if you're in an interpersonal industry (which is any industry in which people are involved), it's a muscle you absolutely need to strengthen. Years ago I read a statistic: Dentists with good chairside manner are five times less likely to be sued than those without it. The lesson? Be a likable person. I know the names of all my residents and their families. I commit details to memory. It's not about impressing people, it's about making them feel *seen*. It humanizes you to them and them to you and that alone is vital to a successful communication of any kind. I've even taken it a step further. Over the past twenty years, I have learned a lot of sign language and Spanish. I've noticed when you take time to literally learn someone else's language, you're demonstrating that you care enough to invest in them and their culture. Language is the inroad to culture. As Chris Voss says, when you speak someone's language, you're essentially knowing their religion. This tool builds incredible bridges.

Everything I've shared here—the importance of empathy, extreme ownership, and finding the Black Swan—comes down to one thing: *human connection*. People want to feel heard, understood, and valued. When you master the art of listening, adapting, and speaking their language, you don't just win negotiations; you build trust through integrity. And integrity is the foundation of every strong relationship, every solid deal, and every great leader. Many police agencies, such as the Missouri State Highway Patrol, want to break you down and rebuild you, pour you into their mold and shape you how they see fit. This usually happens in the six months it takes to go through the academy. What ended up happening in my situation is that they certainly broke me down and reshaped me but did so indirectly, in a much better way that took me the better part of a decade to see. It's a failure I am forever grateful for.

ENDNOTE:

1.   Jocko Willink and Leif Babin, Extreme Ownership (St. Martin's Press, 2015).

About Cal

Cal Hutson is an accomplished entrepreneur and business leader whose path to business ownership was unplanned. In 2007 an unexpected opportunity led him to pursue entrepreneurship, and he has since become deeply involved in business development, management, and leadership. Over the years, Cal has founded and led several companies across diverse industries, ranging from screen printing to assisted living. His success is attributed to a strong focus on innovation, operational efficiency, and fostering collaboration within teams.

Cal holds a bachelor's degree in communication studies from the University of Missouri-Kansas City (UMKC), where he gained a solid grounding in business principles that complement his hands-on experience in building and scaling organizations. His leadership approach emphasizes inspiration and empowerment, cultivating environments that encourage creativity and drive high performance.

Cal's approach to business is driven by a strong belief in continual improvement and adaptability. He understands that the key to success in any venture lies not only in seizing opportunities but also in navigating the inevitable challenges that arise. This mindset has allowed him to consistently grow and evolve with each company he leads. He is passionate about building teams that share his vision and fostering a culture of mutual respect and accountability. Cal's emphasis on mentorship and developing leadership potential within his teams has been crucial in scaling operations and achieving long-term success. His hands-on approach ensures that he remains closely involved in all aspects of his businesses, from strategy to day-to-day operations. Whether through technology adoption, process optimization, or employee development, Cal is always looking for innovative ways to improve and stay ahead in an ever-changing business landscape. This commitment to excellence drives him to continually push the boundaries of what's possible.

Beyond business, Cal is an avid baseball fan, struggles mightily to play the guitar, and is a committed reader of personal development literature, always seeking ways to refine his skills and mindset. He is also a devoted family man, who enjoys spending quality time with his wife, Malonda, and their three children, who all share a passion for theater. As he continues to expand his entrepreneurial ventures, Cal remains focused on creating long-term value for the companies he leads while furthering his personal and professional growth.

CHAPTER 8

WRITE IT BEFORE YOU WING IT

Life by Design

By Ned Markey

I was flying at sixteen thousand feet, in the clag, and night was falling over the Wyoming mountains when I realized we were flying into a thunderstorm. We were almost there, and the storm was moving over our destination much more quickly than I had thought.

The first thing you learn as a pilot is to always have an escape plan. The second thing you learn? The day you don't have one is the day you need it the most. We were on our way to our vacation home in Wyoming, and a case of "get there-itis" had lured me into thinking I could beat the approaching storm. I was wrong.

Inside the cloud, visibility was zero, and I was navigating solely by the aircraft's instruments. Night was falling, the weather at my destination was still suitable for landing, and my alternate airport was now behind us. We continued. Strike one. Sleet started sticking to the wings, and ice pellets bounced off the windshield like marbles, making it nerve-rackingly loud in the cabin. I glanced back at my wife and daughters, and felt a lump form in my throat. They were trusting me to fly us through this. The only plan left was to descend out of the bottom of the clouds. With the mountains directly below us, Salt Lake Center (Air Traffic Control) could not allow that. I was out of back up plans. Why had I misjudged the speed of the storm on the radar? Why did I allow myself to get boxed in like this?

Suddenly we broke out of the cloud on the backside of the storm, and I looked down to see an airport. I canceled my instrument clearance, pulled the power, and spiraled down through the hole in the clouds. We were able to land safely. It took my heart a few hours to stop racing, but I learned something important—you don't rise to the level of your hopes; you fall to the level of your preparation. And life works the same way.

Designing your life is a lot like a pilot creating a flight plan and mapping out a trip—you don't just hop in the cockpit and go. You start with a destination in mind. Then you chart the best route to get there, factoring in possible obstacles and fuel stops along the way. A good flight plan doesn't guarantee a smooth ride, but it gives you direction, contingency plans, and the confidence to successfully navigate whatever comes up.

If you think about what a script is, it's essentially a plan. It's a collection of words to say in a certain order, a kind of road map. I was once at a Broadway performance of The Music Man in which Hugh Jackman was performing the role of Dr. Harold Hill. It was the scene where Mayor Shinn was yelling in Dr. Harold Hill's face. You could see the spit flying out of the actor's mouth. These guys were in their element until Hugh busted out laughing. The whole show stopped. He broke character and laughed in front of the whole audience. We got quite a kick out of it but probably because he's one of the very best in the business, and we witnessed him mess up. What would happen if he *wasn't* one of the best and messed up? What if there was no script to follow or if actors went off-script all the time? It wouldn't work. The audience would be annoyed and the show wouldn't make sense. That's how most of us are going through life—without a plan. Most people are ad-libbing as they go and then waking up one day and wondering, "How did I get here?" They are operating without a script! And you can't flip what you don't have.

Designing your life is like writing an exciting script for your very own show. It means being intentional and thinking ahead about where you're going, why it matters, and what resources you'll need to get there. Whether it's a trip, a life plan, or a tough conversation, the one thing you need to know is where you want to land!

PLAN THE ROUTE

I'll be honest, when I started out, I didn't have much of a flight plan or script for my life.

I was big into sailing and windsurfing in my younger days, and I let the wind decide where I should go. It felt right at the time. I wasn't in a cubicle wearing an uncomfortable suit. I was free!

I took a position in the hospitality industry in Aspen, Colorado and spent a year there as a mountain biker/ski bum. I enjoyed the young community but was shocked to learn that so many people had something called a "trust fund." I wasn't sure what that was, so I called my mom and asked if I had one. She laughed! I eventually landed a job as the food and beverage director at a new hotel in Bellingham, Washington, where I met my wife. I lived on a sailboat and spent my days off sailing the San Juan and Canadian Gulf Islands with Molly. I thought maybe we were living the dream but the older I got, the more I realized the hard truth—I was in an industry with long hours, low pay, and no clear path to growth. I wanted to marry Molly, and that meant it was time to chart a new course.

Then one winter break, I went to visit my parents and my dad, an orthopedic surgeon, asked me if I wanted to watch him perform a knee surgery. Always up for hanging out with him, it was an easy yes. It turned out that his assistant got sick at the last minute. A phone call to the patient's family later and I was scrubbed in, holding a camera in the operating room. That moment, staring at the inside of someone's knee, I made a decision. I didn't want to work for someone else. I wanted control over my time and my future. Dentistry checked every box—science, business, helping others and the ability to own my destiny.

So I flipped my script and went back to school. It was extremely challenging, but it was part of the flight plan now, so I was determined to stay the course. After studying at Columbia University in New York City, we moved upstate for dental school. Then, we spent several years in Pittsburgh for my specialty training in pediatric dentistry and eventually moved to Wisconsin to settle near family. Every move was intentional. Every turn plotted. It soon hit me though that I could only see so many kids per day. Even with all that schooling, my own dental practice, and what most people would define as success, I was still trading time for money. I wanted more than that, so, I started buying real estate all over the country. I was determined to build something that would generate revenue on autopilot. Today, my family and I are fortunate enough to fly in our own plane and visit our vacation rental homes whenever we can. It wasn't luck. It was in the plan.

That's the difference between flying aimlessly and charting your course. Know where you're going. Know *why* you're going. And have a map to get there.

DO A PREFLIGHT (PREPAREDNESS) CHECK

As a pilot, you wouldn't depart without checking your fuel, planning your route, and packing what you need. In life one of the most important skills you can pack is empathy. Empathy gets you where you want to go. Without it you're flying blind.

I often, half-jokingly, tell my dental assistants, "Kids are terrorists, and we don't negotiate with terrorists." But the truth is, in pediatric dentistry your life is a constant negotiation. I've heard it all. "If I can go to the bathroom, *then* I'll sit in the chair." The game never ends. My toughest negotiation over the years? A four-year-old who came in convinced we were going to "torture" him. Why? Because his brother told him so. The second he saw my assistant, he bolted—straight up into the treehouse in our lobby. Kicking, crying, fighting.

Here's the thing: If I went in there tough, that kid would've burned the place down emotionally. Instead, I packed what I needed—tactical empathy. I spotted his Spiderman shoes. "I *love* Spiderman," I said. "Is he your favorite?" His eyes lit up. "Yeah! He saves people!" Boom. There it was. Connection. From there it was simple: Mirroring. Labeling. Every move designed to lower his guard. I made him the hero of his own story. I let him *win*—by choosing to sit in that chair.

"But I'm scared," he said.

"Scared?" I asked.

"You're going to give me shots and yank my teeth out."

"Yank your teeth out?" I repeated.

"That's what my brother told me."

"Your brother?" I asked.

"Yeah. My brother told me it was going to hurt!"

"I'm not sure what dentist your brother went to, but it wasn't me! I won't hurt you! Let me show you what we're going to use." I picked up my mirror and held it in front of him. He was momentarily distracted from his fear.

And when it was time to numb him? He didn't even flinch. Because by that time, he trusted me. Here's the lesson—whether it's a dental chair, a business deal, or your own family—empathy is your fuel. You can't fly without it. You don't win by forcing cooperation. You win by understanding what's driving the other side, meeting them there, and guiding them where they need to go. That's strategic empathy. And it works—every time.

ADJUST MID-FLIGHT—EYES ON THE GOAL

The thing about flying—and life—is that you can chart what seems to be the perfect course and still need to adjust. Winds change. Storms roll in, and if you're locked into one way of getting there, you might not make it. If you've got your chart and know where you're headed, you can be flexible and still land where you planned. That's exactly what my family and I had to do when we embarked on a mission trip to Panama. I often take my wife, kids, and even my employees on mission trips. We've flown to the Dominican Republic, Mexico, St. Lucia, and impoverished parts of the US where people can't afford dental care.

In Panama we worked in Bocas del Toro, a string of remote islands on the Caribbean side. It's beautiful but about as far off the grid as you can get and not entirely safe. I remember growing my hair long before that trip so I didn't look like a guy who had money and his own airplane!

We operated from a small island that had no roads, no running water, no electric grid, and no garbage service. At base all we had was a cistern, solar panels, battery banks, and forty-foot dugout canoes. The cots we slept in had full enclosure bug nets. My daughters thought they were fancy beds like in the Disney princess movies. We loaded portable dental chairs and supplies and motored across the water from island to island. The indigenous people we were treating lived in extreme poverty. There were no cars, no phones, just families trying to survive.

And none of that shook us. We encountered language barriers, poverty, brutal conditions, and we simply adjusted. You see, we knew our mission. We were there to help. With our eyes on the goal, we sailed with the wind, not against it. When supplies ran out, or we didn't have what we needed, we adjusted the flight plan and improvised. I watched my kids playing with the children there even though they spoke different languages. It was beautiful to see that the connection of friendship didn't require words, just presence, empathy and the willingness to meet people where they are.

Those people had nothing and yet they were happy and grateful. That trip made us realize that happiness in life isn't found in what you collect; It's found in who you connect with. And just like flying, if you stay locked on your mission, you can adjust to whatever comes your way and still land where you're supposed to. That's life by design.

LAND THE PLANE—FOR NOW

I've designed my life to be exactly that—*designed*. I've crafted a flight plan for my life that allows me to spend time with my wife and kids, travel the world, give back, and build wealth through businesses and real estate all over the country. It didn't happen because I got lucky—but because I thought it through. I picked a destination, mapped the route, and made sure I had the "supplies" I needed to reach my destination. And the truth is, I'm always revising the flight plan. Every good pilot knows that the wind can change at any moment. What worked for this leg of the trip might not get you through the next. That shift—from ski bum and hospitality kid to dentist, business owner, and investor—didn't happen by chance. It happened because I had a bigger vision and I adjusted mid-flight, when the moment called for it.

That's why I ask my older high school patients, "What do you want to do when you grow up?" I want to challenge them to think bigger. And when they tell me, "I'm not sure yet," I tell them, "I'm not sure yet either, but I'm doing this for now!" I know dentistry isn't my final landing spot. I have other passions as well and will likely not be practicing dentistry forever. I'm great at what I do, and I love it, but there are more adventures and runways ahead.

And that's the point. Life by design means you stay in the pilot's seat. You pick the destination, you adjust when the skies change, but you never stop flying the plane. The goal is to land where you planned—not where the wind happens to push you.

It's no different in business and negotiation. You walk into every deal with a clear target—know where you're trying to land. But you stay flexible because the conversation, like the weather, can change fast. You adjust, navigate around the weather but you keep your eye on the goal. That's how you close the deal, win the client, or grow the business—by knowing exactly where you're going.

So ask yourself, "What's next? Where am I going? How will I get there?" The most dangerous thing you can do is take off without a plan—and end up somewhere you never intended.

Design your life. Chart the course. Adjust as needed. And when the time comes—land the plane. Until it's time to take off again for the next adventure—life by design.

About Ned

Ned Markey is an accomplished board-certified pediatric dentist, aviator, entrepreneur, real estate investor, and adventurer who lives at the intersection of precision and purpose. Whether navigating the skies or guiding a child through their first dental visit, he brings calm, clarity, and connection to every moment.

Ned spent his young-adult years as a ski bum in Aspen, Colorado; living on a sailboat in the San Juan Islands, Washington; and studying at Columbia University in New York City and abroad in Valparaiso, Chile— experiences that shaped his global perspective and deepened his passion for people, culture, and purposeful living.

With a heart for service, Ned has provided missionary dental care in underserved communities both in the US and abroad. His work in developing countries has deepened his belief that dignity and empathy are universal languages—and that healthcare, when delivered with compassion, can be a powerful bridge to hope and healing.

As a loving husband and father of three, his greatest calling is at home— where faith and intentionality shape the way he leads in marriage, parenting, business, and everyday life. He believes in living a *life by design*, not by default, and credits God as his copilot in all things.

His journey has taught him that empathy, planning, and preparation are essential tools—not just in practice but in relationships and leadership. Drawing from these disciplines, he is passionate about equipping and inspiring younger generations to thrive in every area of life, such as marriage, finances, parenting, and business.

When he's not treating patients, flying airplanes, or building businesses, you'll find him mountain biking, snowboarding, sailing, or investing in meaningful conversations that point others toward purpose.

He lives each day with the goal of inspiring others to live lives of impact—boldly, faithfully, and by design.

Connect with him on Instagram: @LifeByDesign_NedMarkey.

CHAPTER 9

SPEAKING THEIR LANGUAGE

The Power of Seeing, Listening, and Understanding

By Fran Malkin

The first thing I noticed was his silence. It was not the typical teenage variety, the kind born from boredom. This was heavier, as if he'd sealed himself inside a vault no one had the combination to. He sat in the back corner of my classroom, head down, and dragged a paper clip across his wrist. He did no work, answered no questions.

The other teachers didn't seem phased. "That's just the way he is," they said. "Don't waste your energy. Float him through." It seemed to be an agreed-upon truth that this was all he'd ever be. Unreachable. Forgotten. I knew that floating wasn't an option I could live with. I also knew that talking at him would go nowhere. A lecture wouldn't unlock whatever door he'd bolted shut. I had never been interested in standing at the front of the room, spitting out facts, and I didn't believe in one-sided conversations. Teaching, to me, had always been about meeting people where they are, building trust, and learning from one another.

So when exam day came, I slid a folded note onto his desk. "I know you won't take this test," I wrote. "And that's OK. But I also know something isn't right. I'm here if you need help." When the bell rang and the room emptied, he came up to my desk and in a voice that was almost a whisper said, "I've been like this for over a year—you're the first person who's offered help." I walked with him down to the social worker's office. I remember how quiet that walk was and how strange it was to feel responsible for someone

I'd barely exchanged words with. But that's the thing about real communication—it has very little to do with how much you say and everything to do with how deeply you listen, even when no one's speaking.

Days passed. Then weeks. He never came back to school. I had never found out what happened to him, but years later I received a letter from him. He said he hadn't learned a single word of Spanish, yet Spanish class saved his life. He said someone had finally heard him. And that made all the difference. He was married now and a father. He was going back to school. He was *alive*.

That moment became the blueprint for everything I would come to believe about human connection, whether I was standing in front of a classroom, sitting across from a client, or navigating a high-stakes sales negotiation. Tactical empathy—real, intentional, practiced empathy—isn't about grand gestures or perfect words. It's about noticing what others overlook and refusing to float anything through without your best effort at resolution.

In the years that followed I would use that skill set every day, because my career took quite a turn when more than sixty people were accidentally killed.

BUILDING TRUST

Sixty-four people lost their lives. Seven hundred fifty more were infected, all because of contaminated steroid injections from a single compounding pharmacy. The 2012 fungal meningitis outbreak traced back to the New England Compounding Center wasn't just a tragedy—it was a wake-up call. The system meant to protect patients had failed them. In response, Congress passed the Drug Quality and Security Act (DQSA), creating a new category of drug manufacturing: FDA-Registered 503B Outsourcing Facilities. For the first time, there was a pathway for high-quality, customized medications to be produced at scale, under strict FDA oversight, without the need for patient-specific prescriptions.

It was the start of something new. But new makes people

nervous. At the same time, my husband, a healthcare entrepreneur, saw another crisis brewing—this time in dermatology. Insurance companies were increasingly classifying dermatologic treatments as "cosmetic," denying coverage, delaying care, and dictating what doctors could prescribe. Providers were backed into corners. Patients were paying the price. While dermatological issues may not be physically life-threatening, they took a deep toll on mental health, especially for kids. We saw this as both a problem and an opportunity to help people, so my husband launched SKNV, an FDA-Registered 503B Outsourcing Facility designed to return control to the people who should have had it all along—doctors!

We focused on dermatology because it was being overlooked. We focused on quality because lives had already been lost when shortcuts were taken. And we focused on access because patients deserve to receive help without having to blow through their savings to get it.

Today, SKNV manufactures over 120 customized topical dermatology medications treating seventeen disease states. We give providers the ability to dispense medications directly from their offices. No insurance interference. No prior authorizations. No medication substitutions. Just personalized care delivered immediately.

It sounds simple. It sounds obvious. But new solutions don't sell themselves.

The FDA has been around for over a century. 503B Outsourcing Facilities? A little more than a decade. SKNV? Even younger. And when you're new, you're unknown. When you're unknown, you're questioned. And when you're questioned, you better know how to communicate, not just clearly—but strategically.

That's where I come in. After twenty years in education, I understood that knowledge alone doesn't change minds. People don't buy products. They buy *trust*. And trust is built through connection—through listening first, asking better questions, and understanding what the person on the other side of the conversation actually needs, not just what you're hoping to sell them. In short, this work required tactical empathy. Not sympathy or generic friendliness, but the ability to step inside someone else's world, see the obstacles from their side of the table, and guide them to a solution that feels as good to them as it does to you. It wasn't just the patients who needed care. It was the providers who had been ignored, overruled, and underserved by a system that made practicing good medicine harder than it needed to be.

My job became twofold: educate my team so they could educate our providers, so the providers could better care for their patients, and build relationships strong enough to overcome the natural skepticism that comes with anything new, no matter how desperately it's needed. Negotiation isn't just about getting to yes. It's about understanding why the answer was almost no. And in a young, transformative industry like ours, where the stakes are high and the trust is thin, that skill set isn't optional. It's *survival*.

Don't Sell Them, *See* Them

As our business grew, my husband and I spent a lot of time challenging each other's ideas, pressure-testing strategies, and sharing resources. One of those resources—Chris Voss' *Never Split the Difference*—changed everything.

When I finally read it, something clicked. *Everything* is a negotiation. In a *Black Swan* newsletter article, Sandy Hein wrote, "Negotiation is about communication; negotiation invites communication and collaboration." That hit me. That was exactly what we were trying to do every single day at SKNV: communicate better. Not just pitch products. Not just "sell" but collaborate, communicate, and solve real problems for real people.

So we made 2024 "the SKNV Year of *Never Split the Difference*." We gave the entire sales team the book, held monthly trainings, worked through every concept—tactical empathy, mirroring, labeling, calibrated questions, getting to no, spotting black swans—and connected them directly to how we engage with our dermatology practices, because our job isn't to push products; it's to solve problems. But first, we have to understand what the real problems are. And that starts with listening. Every dermatology practice we work with falls into one—or more—of three buckets:

1. **Clinical pain:** They're frustrated with limited treatment options and see the cracks in the system.

2. **Administrative overload:** They're drowning in prior authorizations and want their office to run smoother.

3. **Financial growth:** They're focused on the bottom line and want to add a unique revenue stream to their practice.

But here's the key: No one's going to hand you that information on a silver platter. You have to earn it. The best negotiators aren't hunters. They're gatherers. Gatherers observe. Gatherers listen. Gatherers wait. In a busy practice where everyone's defensive from years of being pitched, the worst thing you can do is start talking. We're not there to throw out features and benefits. We're there to say, "Look, we get it. We don't know your office yet. But here's what we're seeing at other practices. Insurance headaches. Prior-authorization fatigue. Frustrations with medication access. Does that sound familiar?" Then, stop talking.

Silence is powerful because in that silence they'll start filling the space. They'll tell you what's not working. They'll give you exactly what you need to know to help them and when they realize you're actually listening—not just waiting for your turn to talk—something shifts. Walls come down. Trust starts to build.

Our sales cycle isn't fast. It takes three or four visits, sometimes more. Before we even suggest they stock inventory, we run a medication report from their own EMR to make sure it's a good fit. If it's not, we walk away. In our case we aren't trying to win a negotiation; we are trying to build a partnership. And the foundation of any good partnership is simple: Find the pain, poke it gently, and then be quiet!

Once you've earned their trust by listening, the next step is learning to speak their language so that nothing gets lost in translation and every solution feels as if it was built just for them.

LEARN A NEW LANGUAGE

If you want to build trust, you must learn to speak the language of the person you're talking to. I learned this years ago, long before SKNV, standing in front of a roomful of doctors in a hospital conference room, playing *Simon says*. I was teaching a medical Spanish course funded by a grant after research showed something profound: Patients would rather have their provider try to speak their language—imperfectly—than sit silently behind a translator. It wasn't about flawless grammar or perfect pronunciation. It was about the effort, the connection, and the attempt to meet someone where they are.

One day during an observation, a university leader pulled me aside and said, "I can't believe you got doctors to play Simon says." What she really meant was, "I can't believe you created a space where people let their guard down long enough to actually learn something new."

That moment led me back to school for my doctorate, and eventually into the work I do now—teaching our consultants how to better teach our providers about SKNV. It's the same ripple effect, the same wave of education, empathy, and communication that keeps moving outward.

The best negotiators take time to learn the languages of the people sitting across from them.

I tell our team all the time: "You've got to sit in the scrubs of the dermatologist. Understand their daily headaches. Step into their routines. Feel their friction points."

You see, when we walk into a practice, we're often met with skepticism. Maybe they've been burned by another company making big promises. Maybe they're exhausted by the chaos of insurance. Maybe they're just jaded from years of being sold to.

That's where tactical empathy becomes the most valuable tool we have. We mirror, label, and listen. "It seems like you've been burned before. It sounds like you're skeptical because of that experience. I can absolutely see why you'd feel that way." A provider might say, "This sounds like a good concept, but I don't want to feel like I'm selling to my patients. I'm not a salesperson." We don't argue. We don't dismiss the concern. We speak their language. "Selling?" we ask. "It sounds like you just don't like the idea of charging patients directly for their medication." "That's right," they say, and then we know we've found common ground.

We reflect it back again. "So, it sounds like you're uncomfortable with the idea of handling money and making it feel transactional." And then comes the reframe: "Well, you're not a salesperson. You're a physician. You prescribe treatments, and now you're simply offering your patients the convenience of picking up that treatment in your office instead of waiting at a pharmacy. You're not selling—you're providing care."

That's when the light bulb goes on. You've listened deeply enough, reflected accurately enough, and reframed gently enough that they feel completely understood.

The best negotiators learn, translate, connect, and create a shared language where progress can truly begin.

Flip the Script

For a long time I thought I was a good communicator because I knew what to say. Turns out, the real power came when I learned how to stop saying anything!

Tactical empathy taught me that listening isn't waiting for your turn to speak. It's not nodding along while your mind races ahead to your next point. It's about truly hearing what's being said, what's not being said, and what someone might not even realize they're trying to tell you. When I stopped filling the silence, something surprising happened—people started telling me the truth.

Whether it was a student, a physician, my husband, or my own kids, I noticed the shift. Instead of trying to push, persuade, or rush through the discomfort, I started holding space. I let the quiet hang in the air just a few seconds longer than felt natural. That's what it means to *flip the script*. Instead of trying to convince people, you create space for them to convince themselves. Instead of pushing harder, you pause. Instead of leading with your agenda, you lead with curiosity.

It's never about "winning." It's about caring so deeply that people feel it, whether they're sitting across from you in a boardroom, in a classroom, at a kitchen table, or in a provider's office. Good communication isn't about outtalking, outselling, or outsmarting anyone. It's about out-*caring* them. It's about slowing down long enough to actually hear what the other person is trying to say—beneath the words, beneath the resistance, beneath the doubt. It's about asking yourself every single time you step into a conversation, "Am I here to be right, or am I here to help?"

Whether you're sitting across from a struggling student, a skeptical provider, your own child, or a roomful of hardened decision-makers, the goal is the same: to understand and be understood. It's to create the kind of trust that turns resistance into resolution, skepticism into collaboration, and silence into the start of something real.

The best negotiators, the best educators, the best leaders—they don't force answers; they make space for answers to reveal themselves. When you do that, when you listen deeply enough, care authentically enough and speak the right language, you don't just close deals; you open doors, you solve problems, and you might, without even realizing it, be saving a life.

About Fran

For over thirty years, Fran Malkin has been a dynamic force in education, training, and professional development. With a career spanning both academia and the corporate sector, she has left a lasting impact on countless students, educators, and professionals across industries.

Fran's career began in the classroom, where she spent two decades teaching at both the secondary and collegiate level in private and public institutions. Her ability to inspire, mentor, and shape young minds earned her a reputation as a dedicated and innovative educator. Throughout these formative years, she not only educated young learners but also mentored future teachers, helping to elevate the standards of instruction and learning.

A decade ago, thanks to her husband's entrepreneurial encouragement, Fran transitioned from traditional education to corporate training, bringing her expertise in curriculum development and pedagogy to the healthcare industry. She began working closely with sales consultants and dermatology providers nationwide, applying her deep understanding of learning strategies to empower professionals in the field.

In her current role as vice president of education and development at SKNV, an FDA-Registered 503B Outsourcing Facility in South Florida, Fran leads the charge in designing cutting-edge training programs. She develops and implements educational initiatives that equip SKNV's national sales force with the knowledge and skills necessary to communicate the value of SKNV's customized solutions to their customers. Through her leadership she helps dermatology professionals navigate everyday challenges and optimize patient care.

Whether she is crafting compelling training materials, integrating new learning technologies, or fostering engaging discussions, Fran's approach to education is hands-on, interactive, and forward-thinking. She believes in lifelong learning and is passionate about leveraging modern educational tools to enhance both individual and organizational growth.

Her leadership philosophy is rooted in relationship building—she values mentorship, collaboration, and open dialogue through active listening and tactical empathy, ensuring that every person she teaches or trains feels empowered, confident, and prepared to succeed.

Outside of her professional endeavors, Fran finds joy in exploring the outdoors, particularly spending time at the beach. She has a deep love for travel, and embraces new cultures and experiences wherever she goes. At home she cherishes moments with her husband of nearly twenty-five years, Spencer, and their two adult children, Reid and Ava.

Connect with Fran:
Email: fmalkin@sknv.com

CHAPTER 10

BRACING FOR IMPACT WITH EMPATHY

By Phillip W. Koontz

"It's cancer."

The doctor's words echoed in my mind as I pushed through the obstacle, muscles aching, the air biting against my skin. Pain was normal. Pain was expected. But not this kind of pain. Not this kind of fight.

I was in the middle of BUD/S—the most grueling military training on earth from which Navy SEALs are born. It is six months of training designed to break you before forging you into something stronger. The first phase—the weeding-out phase—was where most men quit. We started with 223 guys, and by the time we finished the first phase, only twenty-nine remained. I was one of them.

I was tired but proud, having just earned the right to move forward, but when I got home to our little apartment in Imperial Beach, my wife, Danielle, was in pain. She had been experiencing a dull, persistent ache in her body. A few days later, on a rare weekend off, we drove to the hospital together, and hours later our world shattered. Stage IV metastatic breast cancer. It had already spread to her bones, her sternum, and twenty-six lymph nodes from her waist up. She was twenty-eight. I was twenty-six. We had been married for six months. And just like that, every dream we had of a family and a future was ripped from our hands.

In BUD/S, pain is a test. It's the tax you pay for greatness. But this wasn't a pain I could outlast. This wasn't a battle I could win with sheer willpower. I was a warrior, a protector—trained to break men and survive the impossible. I wanted to crawl inside her body and fight for her. Rip the disease apart with my bare hands. But this was a battle I couldn't fight. I could only sit on the sidelines and watch. That's when I learned the most valuable lesson of my life: the power of empathy.

There's a big difference between sympathy and empathy. Sympathy is looking down at someone in the hole and saying, "I'm sorry you're down there." Empathy is climbing down into the hole with them, feeling their pain, standing with them in their darkest hour.

I had to learn to sit with Danielle in her suffering—not to fix or fight but to be fully present. And at the same time, I had to compartmentalize to survive BUD/S while my world crumbled around me. For four years she fought harder than anyone I'd ever seen. And when she passed on February 13, 2008, I was by her side. I had survived the most brutal training on earth, but nothing compared to the battle she fought. And nothing compared to what she taught me.

I learned the power of presence. I learned that true strength isn't about domination but surrender. That we are capable of far more than we ever believe. That faith doesn't get you around trouble; it gets you *through* it. And that empathy—real, tactical empathy—isn't weakness. It's the most powerful weapon we have in our arsenal.

The Language of Leadership

Today, I stand on stages as a best-selling author, keynote speaker, and life coach. I mentor Special Forces candidates, run leadership webinars, and work with the Anti-Trafficking Bureau—a non-profit that rescues and protects children trapped in the nightmare of sexual exploitation. But none of that would mean anything if I hadn't learned one of the most critical skills in leadership: empathetic communication.

I couldn't communicate with my wife the same way I communicated with my brothers in the Teams. A battlefield mindset—direct, aggressive, mission focused—wasn't what she needed. She didn't need orders. She didn't need solutions barked at her. She needed *me*. That was the first lesson: Communication isn't about what's easiest for you; it's about what's effective for *them*. I see this same disconnect everywhere in leadership. Too many people operate with a microwave mentality—quick, transactional, surface-level leadership. Get people in, push them through, check the box. *Ding!* They're done. But it doesn't stick. It's wide but not deep.

I don't lead like that. I believe in the electric cooking pot model—low and slow, building something real, taking the time to invest in people, to understand them, to go deep so the impact lasts. The quality is better because the process is better. As leaders we must model the behavior we want to see in others. A culture of authentic leadership takes time to build.

When Danielle was diagnosed, I was standing at a fork in the road. I could get angry and numb the pain with alcohol, medication, and distractions, or I could be an anchor of stability. I chose the second path because leadership isn't always about fixing things—it's about walking with people through their hardest moments by speaking the language they need to hear.

Empathy isn't about feeling sorry for someone. It's about identifying their emotion and connecting with it. No attempting to solve the problem, because sometimes you can't, but as the *means* to truly engage with it.

In the military we carried something called a blood chit, a small document written in multiple languages, promising a reward to anyone who helped a service member in a dire situation. It was a tool for survival, a way to communicate in the language of the people around us. Tactical empathy is the same thing. It's not about how *you* want to communicate; it's about how *they* need to hear it. Leaders who don't understand this fail. They push information instead of building connection. They assume instead of listening. They jump to conclusions without truly empathetically listening to the deeper message. But the best leaders? They take the time. They gain trust. They learn the language. Your clients, your team, and your family—they don't care how much you know until they know how much you care. So take the time. Learn the language of empathy. And once you've mastered the words, master the delivery—use a velvet sledgehammer.

THE VELVET SLEDGEHAMMER

In the SEAL teams, we learn to flip switches fast. One moment you're in a war zone, making life-or-death decisions. The next, you're home, sitting at the dinner table, expected to be present, and normal. But flipping that switch isn't always immediate. When I came home from deployments in 2006 and 2008, I struggled. I was carrying the battlefield with me. And there were moments when I lost my cool with my wife and others around me. I defaulted to anger and raw intensity. But as things started to unravel, I had to learn that not every problem is solved with a sledgehammer.

Most of us SEALs are type A personalities, trained to take action and blow through obstacles. Some leaders operate with that same mentality all the time, charging in like a bull in a china shop, swinging a sledgehammer at everything in their path. And there are moments when that approach is necessary. When you need to turn a 747 while taking fire or when decisions could cost lives, you need the blunt-force power of the sledgehammer. You need someone who will get the mission done, no matter what. But that approach rarely works outside of those high-stakes moments. What I had to learn was the power of the velvet sledgehammer.

The velvet sledgehammer is about coming in with that same level of determination, the same goal-oriented mindset, but applying it with a softer, more human approach. It's about recognizing that leadership isn't just about solving problems; it's about leading *people* through those problems. It means humanizing the person in front of you and considering their fears, hopes, and struggles. Instead of demanding compliance, you connect. Instead of barking orders, you ask the right questions. You listen not just to respond but to understand.

In the SEAL teams, I was a breacher. Breachers are the ones tasked with eliminating any obstacle that stands in the way of the mission. A door, a wall, a steel gate—it doesn't matter. A breacher will sledgehammer through, blow through, saw through, or burn through whatever is in front of them to get the team where they need to go. And that's the same mindset many leaders have today. They see an obstacle, and they attack. No hesitation, just brute force. But here's the problem: People aren't doors. You can't just break through them and expect them to function properly on the other side. I learned that the hard way.

When I left the military, I struggled. I was diagnosed with Operator Syndrome, a new medical diagnosis that affects many Special Operators. Years of exposure to explosives caused traumatic brain injury (TBI), and the damage was serious. It came with PTSD, memory issues, and a baseline level of anger that I hadn't yet learned to control. At home there was no mission, and I didn't know how to process that anger anymore. So I kept using the sledgehammer. In the way I spoke, my tone, my body language—all of it carried the same force I had used in combat, and it was damaging my relationships.

I had a come-to-Jesus moment in 2011 and knew I had to change. I had to stop swinging the hammer blindly and start leading with precision. The best leaders understand that it's not just what you say; it's how you say it. You can have the best strategy in the world, but people can't hear you when you're screaming or demanding. They may *listen*, but fear will override their ability to take meaningful action. Fear-based leadership creates short-term compliance but never long-term commitment. So the question is, Are you breaking people down or breaking through to them? The best leaders know when to swing the hammer and when to soften the blow. They know when to push, when to pause, and when to listen. That's the velvet sledgehammer. And that's how you truly get results.

The Bridge to Every Goal

For the last eight years, I've served as a SEAL motivator—mentoring candidates who want to become SEALs, coaching them through the mental and physical demands, and helping them build the mindset required to succeed. It's fulfilling work, not just because I'm giving back but because I know firsthand what it means to have someone in your corner. No one accomplishes anything alone. That's a truth SEAL training reinforces at every level. BUD/S is one of the only programs in the world where officers and enlisted men train side by side. Why? Because the Navy understands that trust, not rank, determines who survives.

If we're taking enemy fire, the junior enlisted guy might be the first to see the threat. He can't wait for permission to act. He gets on the radio, makes the call, and saves lives. That's leadership in action. That's tactical decision-making. And it works because we train our people to lead by serving the mission, not their fears or ego. One of the first lessons I teach SEAL candidates is this: *Get your eyes off yourself and onto your teammates.* BUD/S divides us into six- or seven-man boat crews, grouped by height. We carry inflatable boats on our heads, through the sand, through the waves, through exhaustion. And here's the reality: If you're only thinking about how much you hurt, you're already failing. The men who survive don't focus on their own suffering—they focus on the guy next to them. Who's struggling? Who needs encouragement? Whom can I support? That shift in focus from *self-preservation* to *serving others* is the key to making it through the hardest training in the world, because when we help others push through, we push through ourselves.

People hear the word *negotiation* and picture a long table surrounded by hard-nosed executives each pushing their own agenda. But the best negotiators—whether in business, on the battlefield, or in life—aren't focused on winning. They're focused on *serving*. Why? Because people respond to authenticity. If you're just trying to extract value, they'll resist you. But if you genuinely care and seek to understand what the other person needs, you'll find common ground faster, lower their defenses, and open the door to real influence. At the core of tactical empathy is humility. Not thinking *less* of yourself but thinking about yourself *less*.

THE TRUE STRENGTH OF MENTAL TOUGHNESS

Ask anyone to describe a Navy SEAL, and most people will use words like "tough" or "strong." And it's true. We are trained to be the toughest, strongest warriors in the world, both mentally and physically. Yet what I've learned is that mental toughness is not aggression and force. It's *discernment*. It's knowing when to push and when to pause. It's the ability to step outside yourself, read the situation, and respond in the way that serves the mission, the team, and the goal.

True toughness is the ability to regulate emotions, overcome adversity, and persist in the face of challenges—not through brute force, but through intentional, controlled action. And here's the part most people miss: Mental toughness and positivity aren't opposites. They are directly correlated. We tend to think of toughness as hardened, calloused, and indifferent. But the strongest people—the ones who endure, inspire, and lead, aren't the ones who detach from emotion. They are the ones who *harness* it. They don't see hardship as insurmountable; they see it as an opportunity. They don't dwell on failure; they extract lessons and move forward with clarity and confidence. This is the same mindset that gets candidates through BUD/S. It's the same approach that makes negotiation effective. It's what allows leaders to wield the velvet sledgehammer, and at its core it's about serving others.

A leader focused only on themselves will crumble under pressure. A negotiator focused only on their own gain will lose the deal. A person consumed by their own struggle will never see the path forward. But when you shift the focus—when you lift up the people in your boat crew, communicate with tactical empathy, and lead with humility rather than ego—everything changes. Mental toughness isn't about controlling reality. It's about facing it with the kind of mindset that makes resilience possible. And that's what separates those who break from those who break through.

About Phillip

Phillip W. Koontz is a distinguished US Navy SEAL combat veteran, keynote speaker, and best-selling author. With a career spanning over a decade in the military, Phillip has dedicated his life to serving his country and inspiring others through his experiences and insights. His journey began when he enlisted in the Navy, where he underwent rigorous training to become a member of the elite SEAL teams. Throughout his service he participated in numerous high-stakes missions, demonstrating exceptional leadership, resilience, and commitment to excellence.

After his honorable discharge from active duty, Phillip transitioned into the realm of pastoral ministry, where he focused on the spiritual aspects of life. After four years as a Community Life pastor in the Vineyard church Phillip transitioned into motivational speaking and business coaching.

Throughout his career in public speaking, Phillip has made a significant impact on audiences across the world. His unique perspective, shaped by the challenges and triumphs of military and personal life, allows him to connect with individuals from all walks of life. Phillip's speeches focus on themes of leadership, positivity, conflict resolution, preparedness, and personal growth, empowering others to overcome obstacles and achieve their goals.

In addition to his speaking engagements, Phillip is passionate about mentoring future SEAL candidates. He helps train and prepare his candidates for the world's toughest military training. This is one way he volunteers his time and gives back to the NSW community.

Phillip is also an avid advocate for veterans. His commitment to giving back to the community is evident in his involvement with various organizations that assist veterans and their families. He believes that the lessons learned in the military—such as discipline, perseverance, and the importance of camaraderie—are invaluable tools that can be applied in everyday life and in the business world.

In his new book, Phillip shares powerful stories from his military career, along with practical strategies for leadership and personal development. His candid reflections and actionable insights serve as a guide for anyone looking to enhance their leadership skills and foster a mindset of resilience.

When he is not speaking or writing, Phillip enjoys spending time with his family, exploring the great outdoors, and continuing his lifelong journey of learning. He resides in Colorado Springs, Colorado, with his wife and children, where he remains dedicated to inspiring the next generation of leaders.

CHAPTER 11

THE POWER OF PURE INTENTION

By Nick Nanton

I was on my back in the dentist's chair, mouth wide open and instruments poking at my cheek, yet all I could think about was the awkward conversation I could no longer avoid. We were finally making it happen. A man I had admired for years had agreed to partner with me and let me tell his story in a documentary, and it was finally coming together—with one glitch. I wanted to introduce him to the writer we'd used for our last film. This guy was a total pro and produced an amazing final product. My new partner took the meeting, said it went great, but then told me he wanted to have a few more conversations before deciding. I thought, "Why? I just gave you the guy you need."

Weeks passed, and he started sending me names of people who had impressive résumés, but all from traditional feature films. This wasn't a fictional feature film but a gritty, true documentary that would require a different type of vision, courage, and artistry. Meanwhile, the clock was ticking, and momentum was running dry. I was stuck between two uncomfortable places—respecting a legend's process and opinion, and honoring what I *knew* to be right.

So, there I was, sitting in the dentist's office, anxiety building up, and it hit me that I needed to grow some guts and make the call. I opened with a no-oriented question (hey, I learned from Chris Voss too, so I had some solid tools in my toolbox): "Is now a bad time?" I asked.

He said no. Then, "Would it offend you if I was direct but kind?"

What I said next took more courage than I expected. "Look, one of the things people love about me is that I'm always open to new ideas, always learning. But sometimes that humility makes me hesitate to lean in to my own strengths. So, I'm making a request—not out of ego but out of experience. I've vetted this writer. I trust him. I believe he's the right guy. I'm asking you to go with my recommendation." He paused, then said, "I trust you. Let's get started."

That moment taught me something I'll never forget. It wasn't about winning or being right. It was about leading with *intention*. When I entered the conversation, my intention wasn't to override my partner's opinion or process. My intention was to serve the mission. To put the best person in the job and protect the vision we were building. And that's the thing about intention—when it's clear, aligned, and pure, it's the most powerful communication tool there is.

INTENTION IS *EVERYTHING*

A knife can be a life-saving tool or a life-ending weapon. Same object. Same material. The difference? *Intention.* The words "I don't want to live without you" can be the sweetest line of a wedding vow—or the start of a true-crime docuseries. Again, same words, different outcomes. *Intention makes all the difference.*

Intention is the precursor to outcome. It's the filter everything else flows through, especially empathy. Before you can employ tactical empathy, you need to be grounded in what you're actually trying to accomplish. Are you trying to connect or control? Heal or win?

That call with my new partner wasn't just a pivotal moment in getting his story told—it was a pivot point for me personally because it forced me to stand inside a conversation I would've avoided in the past.

See, I used to be the guy who wouldn't have the conversation at all. If there was tension or the risk of hurting someone's feelings,

I'd just disappear. You just wouldn't hear from me again. No confrontation. No conflict. I'd tell myself I was "keeping the peace," but really I was just dodging discomfort.

This situation helped me reframe all that. I realize that when you enter a conversation with clear, respectful *intention*, it doesn't have to be combative—it can be clarifying. Even connective. It works both ways too. Sometimes someone in my life will say something total harmless, and instantly I'm spinning a whole story in my head about what they *meant* by it.

But I've learned to pause and ask, "Hey, what was your intention in telling me that?"

Nine times out of ten, they weren't trying to jab me. They just noticed something and said it. That one question prevents me from spiraling and helps me reconnect to reality—and to those people around me who care about me and whom I care about, because when you know someone's intention, you can respond instead of react.

Author Bryant McGill said, "Every journey begins with the first step of articulating the intention, and then *becoming* the intention."[1] I've found that's especially true in business. When I walk into a meeting or a pitch—whether it's with a billionaire such as Richard Branson, or a celebrity client such as Kathie Lee Gifford, or a nonprofit I believe in—I don't lead with credentials or clout. I don't say, "Here's what I've done; here's what I deserve; here's why you should work with me." I walk in with this mindset: "This person owes me nothing. They've made it this far just fine without Nick Nanton. But what might it look like to enrich their life if we do something cool together?" That's *intention*.

And when intention is aligned with empathy, it becomes the most powerful form of communication there is. It's how you have hard conversations without breaking trust. It's how you negotiate with power and humility. It's how you lead with service, even in high-stakes scenarios. Be clear on your intention before you open your mouth, because intention isn't just where communication starts; it's what gives it meaning.

Permission to Lead

Not long ago I hired a consultant to help with a specific area of my business—an area that's both mission-critical *and* deeply personal to me: partnerships. Now, partnerships are how we move the needle. They're how we make real impact. I've built a career on creating meaningful collaborations with celebrity experts—not gimmicky exchanges but real alliances where we do great things *together*. That's the heartbeat of my business. But finding the right partners? That's getting harder.

So, I brought in a consultant who came highly recommended and who specializes in connections and dealmaking. Early on he started walking me through his system, and the more we talked, the more I realized that his definition of *partnership* wasn't the same as mine.

His approach leaned transactional—"You promote mine; I'll promote yours." That's not how I roll. To me, a true partnership isn't a trade. It's a *mission alignment*. It's "Let's do something together that neither of us could do alone." I'm not looking for swaps. I'm looking for synergy.

Still, I stayed open. Maybe there was gold there I just wasn't seeing. Then he said, "Let me teach you how to give a really good elevator pitch—how to help someone understand what you need."

And that's when I felt it. That inner tension. That old familiar voice: "Don't say anything. Just be nice. Let him do his thing. Sit through it. Smile." But I'd learned better. So I said the line that's saved me from countless wasted hours and missed opportunities: "Would it offend you if I was direct but kind?" He said no. So I told him, "Listen, I get that some people need that from you, and I respect that. But I have a lot of experience working with partners, and getting them to see the value of what I do isn't an issue. I know how to explain what I do and what I need. That's not what I hired you for. What I really need help with is finding more *of the right kind* of people to partner with."

He didn't flinch, just said, "No problem at all. Let's move to that." That was it.

We pivoted, got to the real work, and best of all—we got to the outcome *faster* than if I'd tiptoed around the truth, trying not to offend. In the past I probably would've stayed quiet and sat through two hours of something I didn't need (most likely being very distracted), all to avoid confrontation. But that's not leadership. That's self-abandonment.

See, there's a way to stand in your expertise *without* ego. To be humble *without* shrinking. To be kind *without* being a pushover. The key is *intention*. My intention wasn't to make him feel small or to flex my résumé. It was to respect *both* of us—his time and mine. To honor the value I bring *and* the value I was seeking. And that's the balance we're all trying to strike in business, in life, in leadership.

When you approach people with *clear, respectful intention*, you can say the hard thing, ask for what you actually need, and still build trust along the way. If your intention is rooted in clarity, service, and respect, then being direct isn't confrontation—it's leadership.

Run Your Intention Through a Rinse Cycle

It's one thing to talk about intention in business or negotiation. But if you really want to test the purity of your intention, try applying it in situations where your assumptions have been running the show for years.

I'll never forget the first time I saw a trafficking victim on the street. To be honest, she looked exactly like what I'd been taught to believe a prostitute looked like. That was the story I'd been handed growing up. That was the assumption. And it was dead wrong. What I didn't know—and what I've come to understand through the lens of documentary filmmaking and storytelling—is that most of these individuals aren't breaking the law by choice. They're being forced into it. Some are being trafficked through addiction, with predators using substances as leverage. Others are being threatened and are held hostage by fear and shame.

If you start digging into the data—and more importantly, the stories—you find people caught in webs of coercion, sextortion, or fake relationships turned dangerous, young kids who were manipulated into sending a photo, only to be blackmailed into sending more, doing more, until they're trapped. Is every case like that? No. But enough are. That's why we have to be willing to ask ourselves, "What if my assumptions are wrong?"

From a documentary standpoint, I've learned to look deeper. Many of these people didn't make intentionally bad choices. They made the *best* choice they could at the time with the options in front of them. That changed everything for me. Empathy isn't just about feeling bad for someone. It's about refusing to judge someone whose experience you haven't lived. And believe me, that's not easy. I'm preaching to myself just as much as anyone reading this right now. It's a skill that must be practiced. And in negotiation—in business, in relationships, in leadership—that mindset is *everything*.

If you walk into a room thinking you know who someone is, what they want, or what they're capable of, your intention might *seem* pure—but it's not. It's clouded. Contaminated by unchecked assumptions. The *real* power in empathy is in letting go of the story you walked in with and being willing to hear theirs. That's why in every conversation, whether it's a Hollywood partnership or a documentary interview with a survivor, I try to start from the same place: "What don't I know yet?" When you check your assumptions at the door, your intention becomes clean. When your intention is clean, your communication becomes compassionate. And in a world full of noise, purity of intention is rare, refreshing, and often the key to sealing the deal.

BE TRUE TO THE STORY

At the end of the day everything I've learned about intention has come down to one thing: Am I being true to the story? Whether it's someone else's story or my own, I've had to get brutally honest with myself and ask, "What's my real intention here?" Am I trying to inspire empathy, or avoid discomfort? Am I trying to elevate the truth, or am I sanding off the edges to make it more palatable? Am I honoring their journey or just trying to force a story arc?

As a director, I've been criticized for leaning toward positivity. People say, "Where's the tension? Where's the conflict?" And I get it. I've never liked conflict. I'm not the guy who naturally runs toward the hard parts of the story. But I've learned—*the hard way*—that if you want to inspire real empathy, you can't skip the struggle. People need to see the messy middle. The almosts. The setbacks. The chapters where the hero's not winning. And honestly? That mirrors my own growth.

In every conversation now, whether I'm negotiating a deal, telling a story, or just sitting with a friend, I try to check myself: Is my intention pure? Am I trying to control, impress, or protect? Or am I trying to connect, to serve, to be real? The greatest stories don't follow a straight line. Neither do the greatest lives. And the most meaningful communication doesn't come from polished scripts but from clean intention.

So here's what I know for sure: If you want to influence, lead, or leave a legacy, get clear on your intention before you speak, because intention doesn't just shape your words—it shapes the impact they leave behind.

ENDNOTE

1.   Bryant McGill, *Voice of Reason* (Paper Lyon Publishing, 2012).

About Nick

From the slums of Port-au-Prince, Haiti, with special forces raiding a sex trafficking ring and freeing children, to the Virgin Galactic Space Port in Mojave with Sir Richard Branson, twenty-two-time Emmy Award–winning Director-Producer Nick Nanton has become known for telling stories that connect. Why? Because he focuses on the most fascinating subject in the world: *people*. As an award-winning songwriter, storyteller, and best-selling author, Nick has shared his message with millions of people through his documentaries, speeches, blogs, lectures, songs, and best-selling books. Nick's book *StorySelling* hit The Wall Street Journal Best-Seller List and is available on Audible as an audiobook. Nick has directed more than sixty documentaries and a sold-out Broadway Show (garnering forty-three Emmy nominations in multiple regions and twenty-two wins), including:

- *DICKIE V* (ESPN/Disney+)
- *Rudy Ruettiger: The Walk On* (Amazon Prime)
- *The Rebound* (Netflix)
- *Operation Toussaint* (Amazon Prime)

Nick has shared the stage with, coauthored books with, and made films featuring:

- Larry King
- Kathie Lee Gifford
- Hoda Kotb
- Dick Vitale
- Kenny Chesney
- Magic Johnson
- Coach Mike Krzyzewski
- Jack Nicklaus
- Tony Robbins
- Lisa Nichols
- Peter Diamandis
- And many more

Nick specializes in bringing the element of human connection to every viewer, no matter the subject. He is currently directing and hosting the series *In Case You Didn't Know* (season 1 executive produced by Larry King), featuring legends in the worlds of business, entrepreneurship, personal development, technology, and sports.

Nick's first love has always been music. He has been writing songs for more than two decades, and his songs have been aired on radio across the

United States and in Canada. He is currently ranked in the top 10 percent of songwriters in the world. His songs have been recorded by Lee Brice, Darius Rucker, RaeLynn, Joe Bryson, and many more, and have amassed more than three million streams on Spotify, Apple Music, Pandora, and SoundCloud. He received three Gold records in 2018 for his work with the global touring band A Day to Remember.

Nick has written and/or produced songs that have appeared on the following shows or in promotional commercials for:

- the Fox prime-time series *Glee, New Girl, House,* and *Hell's Kitchen*
- the MLB All-Star Game
- ABC Family's hit series *Falcon Beach*
- the CBS prime-time series *Ghost Whisperer* starring Jennifer Love Hewitt

CHAPTER 12

EMPATHY IN ACTION

Navigating Legacy Negotiations with Tactical Precision

By Amy Peterson

"**T**hey canceled the leases," my husband said.

In that instant, my world collapsed—shattered, like an unexpected death, leaving me stunned, scared, and utterly heartbroken. As I looked out our living room window to the land that stretched beyond it, his words going round and round in my head, it hit me that this land held more than crops—it held our history, our hopes, and our dreams.

Every row we planted, every season we endured was a testament to our shared work ethic and a family legacy. It was our home, and now there was a possibility it would all be stripped away. For twenty-six years my husband and I farmed this land. We didn't just work it—we poured ourselves into it. For fifteen of those we had farmed alongside his grandparents and brother, learning from their hands, sharing their rhythms, believing that this land was a kind of generational promise. My husband had spent years negotiating our leases with his grandfather, and while it wasn't always smooth sailing, those conversations were built on an understanding that we were stewards of something bigger than ourselves.

The sudden loss of my mother-in-law just eighteen months after we were married had shaken the family to its core, and the cords that held the family agreements together began to unravel. You see, in agriculture, landowners usually hold more power. They can find another tenant if they need to, but farmers who have invested in the land don't have that same flexibility.

When my husband's grandfather's health started declining, he had his lawyer and trustees step in, and the lease we had depended on, worked for, and honored was abruptly canceled. It was a decision his grandfather had put in motion not out of malice but out of a rigid adherence to old-fashioned ways. It wasn't just the land we lost—it was trust, it was history, and it was the illusion that hard work and good intentions were enough. Unfortunately, this would not be the last time we faced this issue.

That moment split my life into a before and an after. I grew up in an environment where hard work was just part of life. You didn't complain; you just did what needed to be done. That gave me a strong work ethic, but it also made me believe that if you just worked hard enough, everything would work out.

What I've learned since then is that hard work alone isn't enough. Before, I believed in fairness and in legacy. After, I understood power. I understood that negotiation wasn't just about logic or contracts—it was about *leverage*. And in that moment, we didn't have much of it.

So what do you do when the ground beneath you is ripped away? When the very thing you built your life around is taken without warning?

You plant your feet. You fight for what remains. And you learn that sometimes survival comes from knowing how to stand your ground, how to take up space, and how to steer a negotiation in the direction you need it to go.

WHY LEARNING TO NEGOTIATE IS A NECESSITY

Losing land is one thing. Losing the home that sits in the middle of it is another.

I loved our home—not just the walls or the view from the front porch, but everything it represented. It was the heart of our farm, our family, and our identity. And then, in what felt like an instant, I had to imagine life without it. I had to face the very real possibility that we might have to leave, to start over somewhere new. The thought of being uprooted was devastating. It felt like a divorce—an abrupt separation from something that had shaped me.

But this time, we weren't up against family. With my husband's grandfather gone just a few years later, we found ourselves back at the table with his lawyer and trustees—people with whom we shared no deep past, no blood, and no understanding of the sacrifices we had made—after yet another lease was left to lapse, a familiar tactic that kept them holding all the cards. That's when I realized that negotiation wasn't just a skill for businesspeople in boardrooms. It wasn't just something you used when buying a car or settling a contract. It was survival.

For years I watched my husband navigate lease negotiations. Some were successful. Others collapsed. All of them were draining. Each one took an emotional toll, and each loss felt personal. We were fighting for more than land; we were fighting for our future, our security, our ability to stay rooted. And yet time and again we walked into negotiations without the tools we needed to level the playing field.

Then, at a Women Managing the Farm conference, I sat next to a woman named Jamaca Battin. She told me how her husband had encouraged her to learn negotiation, calling it one of the most valuable skills she could develop. Her words hit me like a wake-up call. It felt like something I was meant to hear.

Not long after, I found myself on a flight from Nashville, sitting next to Craig Williams, the senior VP of sales for Zephyr Gin. He spoke about his own approach to negotiation, how it wasn't just about winning but about understanding leverage, timing, and human psychology. He even scribbled down key strategies on a napkin—a napkin I still have to this day. That conversation solidified something I already knew deep down: Negotiation wasn't just for corporate executives. It touched every industry, every deal, every interaction where something was at stake.

Today, I hold the title of Accredited Land Manager (ALM) with the American Society of Farm Managers and Rural Appraisers (ASFMRA) and co-own multiple agribusiness ventures. But I didn't get here by waiting for fairness to find me. I got here because I learned how to lead tough conversations. I started studying negotiation like my future depended on it—because it did. I dove into Chris Voss' work, watching videos, reading books, and learning the art of tactical empathy. I encouraged my husband to do the same. We had to understand the power plays. We had to learn how to advocate for ourselves, and we did!

With the encouragement of a mentor, Joanna Dahlseid, I now help others develop the confidence to know that they don't have to just accept what's handed to them. They don't have to stay quiet, back down, or hope that someone else will fight for them. They can negotiate. They can lead. And they can do it without losing themselves in the process.

THE POWER OF TACTICAL EMPATHY IN NEGOTIATION

Negotiation isn't just about getting what you want—it's about understanding what the other side needs to hear. It's about making them feel heard, seen, and valued. And sometimes the hardest part of negotiation isn't standing your ground—it's choosing to soften when every instinct tells you to toughen up. Chris Voss really helped me see that.

One defining moment in our fight for the farm came during a meeting with the farm manager and his team. Up until that point, the conversations had been frustrating, full of shifting expectations, vague responses, and a lack of clear direction. Every meeting felt like walking into a storm with no visibility, and I was tired of feeling as if we were the only ones trying to make sense of it all.

I was frustrated, but I had learned the art of tactical empathy—the ability to step into the other person's perspective without losing sight of your own. I had spent so much time assuming their decisions were deliberate roadblocks, but what if they were just as caught in the uncertainty as we were? What if they weren't trying to make things difficult but simply didn't realize how their lack of communication was affecting us? So instead of making demands or airing grievances, I shifted my approach. I framed my concern in a way that invited conversation rather than conflict. "I do a lot better when I understand what's happening," I told him. "When I'm left to assumptions, they tend to be negative. Can we agree that going forward, open communication is our goal?"

That single sentence changed the entire tone of the conversation. Instead of defensiveness, I saw a shift—recognition. The farm manager nodded and agreed. For the first time, it felt as if we weren't just adversaries, but rather two sides trying to solve the same problem. From that moment forward, communication became clearer. There were still challenges, but the dynamic had changed. We had moved from opposition to collaboration. I won't pretend it was easy. In that moment, vulnerability felt like a gamble. It would have been natural to take a hard stance, to push back with demands rather than dialogue. But I knew that doubling down on resistance would only deepen the divide. Instead, I made the harder choice—to be open, to express my frustration in a way that invited resolution rather than retaliation.

That's the thing about tactical empathy—it doesn't mean surrendering. It doesn't mean backing down. It means recognizing that the other side is human too and that understanding their perspective might be the key to unlocking progress.

That one conversation didn't solve everything. There were still setbacks. Still there were miscommunications, still, moments when I had to recalibrate my expectations. But every time I hit a wall, I came back to the same lesson: Negotiation isn't just about what you say—it's about how you make the other party *feel*. When people feel understood, they're more likely to listen. When they feel heard, they're more likely to engage. Tactical empathy isn't about being soft—it's about being strategic. And in negotiations that matter, that's the skill that can turn the tide.

Embrace the Discomfort

Negotiation is like a poker game—sometimes the key to winning is having the patience to sit with an uncomfortable hand rather than folding too soon. Discomfort is an inherent part of any high-stakes conversation. It's often tense, emotional, and uncertain. But instead of rushing to get it over with or giving in just to keep the peace, I've learned to sit with that discomfort and use it to my advantage.

One of my therapists, Ralph Earle, once told me, "You don't have to give away so much of yourself that it leaves you exposed." That stuck with me. I've learned to lead with empathy, to be vulnerable—but not in a way that weakens my position. I can listen, wait, understand, and acknowledge emotions while still standing firm in what I need. That balance is everything.

Negotiation forces you to sit in uncertainty, to confront the unknown, and to acknowledge that you might not walk away with exactly what you want. Early on I believed that winning a negotiation meant securing the best possible outcome—on my terms, in my way. But over time I learned that real success isn't about forcing a specific result. It's about being patient and open to the unexpected.

At first, I resisted that idea. When we were renegotiating land leases, I wanted clarity. I wanted control. I wanted to secure the terms that felt fair, the outcome that felt safe. But the reality of negotiation—especially when you're at a power disadvantage—is that you don't always get exactly what you want in the way you envisioned. That's when sitting in discomfort became a crucial skill. Instead of reacting out of fear, I started asking myself, "What is the ultimate goal here?"

Maybe the goal wasn't just to renew the lease. Maybe the opportunity was in something I hadn't considered—growth, change, new possibilities. When I let go of the idea that success could only look one way, I became more open to what could be rather than clinging to what *was*.

One of the biggest mindset shifts I made was redefining what a "win" looked like. It wasn't always about getting exactly what I wanted. Instead, it became about making the best possible decision given the circumstances—and recognizing the lessons within it. I have learned to ask myself, "Do I actually want this deal? What matters most—price, timing, or the ability to move forward? What is the real win here?"

Discomfort is not the enemy; it's the teacher. The moments that feel the hardest are often the ones where we grow the most. By resisting the urge to react, to rush, or to retreat, I learned to sit with my thoughts, evaluate my position, and make intentional choices.

I realized that negotiation is not just about securing deals—it's about self-awareness. It's about knowing what truly matters, what you're willing to walk away from, and what opportunities might be waiting just beyond your initial expectations.

Now when I walk into a negotiation, I don't just focus on the outcome—I focus on the process—because sometimes the biggest win isn't the deal you make but who you become while you're making it.

THE GIFT IN SKILLING UP

This journey has changed me. Negotiation is no longer something I fear—it's a skill I embrace. What once felt like an intimidating battlefield now feels like an opportunity to strategize, listen, and lead. I've learned to sit in discomfort, ask better questions, and trust the process as solutions emerge. It's no longer just about securing the best deal—it's about making the best decisions for my future, my family, and the legacy we are building.

But this wasn't just about a lease. It was about learning a skill that unlocked a new level of confidence. It was about mastering the art of resilience. And it was about learning the subtle nuances of human behavior as a bridge to building connections rather than divides.

Through tactical empathy I navigated one of the most challenging conversations of my life, not by overpowering the situation but by understanding it. I realized that people don't just respond to logic—they respond to feeling validated.

This shift didn't just affect our business—it transformed my personal life as well. I began to approach difficult conversations with curiosity instead of defensiveness, listening to understand rather than just to respond. That shift has made me a better communicator, a stronger businesswoman, and a more present partner and parent. The tools I learned didn't just give me leverage across the negotiation table. They reshaped how I show up in the world. I now see these deals not as cold transactional meetings but as a chance to turn adversity into opportunity, uncertainty into confidence, and conflict into connection.

All it takes is a willingness to get curious, a desire to keep learning, and the courage to step confidently into the conversations that shape your future, your purpose, and your legacy.

About Amy

Founder of FarmsFull | Accredited Land Manager (ASFMRA) | Negotiation Advocate

Amy Peterson is stepping into her next chapter as the founder of FarmsFull, a consultancy built to ensure everyone in agriculture flourishes—the land, the tenant, and the landlord. Through practical support, personalized consulting, and storytelling, FarmsFull helps people create systems that work, relationships that last, and legacies that matter.

After years of navigating the emotional, financial, and relational complexities of farmland leases and agribusiness management, Amy saw the need for something different—something more human. With deep experience as a Professional Accredited Land Manager (ALM) and a lifetime of lived ag realities, she brings clarity to chaos and language to the often unspoken tensions in agriculture.

FarmsFull isn't just a business—it's a movement rooted in truth telling, stewardship, and connection. And Amy's just getting started. She shares insights about the realities of agriculture, business, and negotiation through her social media platforms, where she connects with others facing similar challenges in the industry.

Follow Amy:
Instagram: www.instagram.com/abcpeterson
Facebook: www.facebook.com/AmyInKansas
Website: www.FarmsFull.com
Email: farmsfullus@gmail.com
X: @kansasfarmgirl1

Amy's journey is one of resilience, problem-solving, and adaptability—qualities that continue to shape her approach to land management and business.

CHAPTER 13

ARM WRESTLING WITH TEXANS

By Marc Rampaul

I n the Permian Basin in West Texas, power wears a cowboy hat, keeps a .45 on its hip, and doesn't take kindly to being told what to do.

The Basin is the largest-producing oil field in the United States made famous by shows such as *Land Man*. Out here, it's not just oil that runs deep—it's pride, ego, and legacy.

Our rig company was young, privately owned, and ambitious. There were three of us—me, Jon, and John. We staked everything on a contract that was supposed to stretch over two years. We'd hauled our brand-new company, every dollar we had, every piece of equipment, and twenty good men two thousand miles from home to Pecos, Texas, because in this business if you want to play big, you can't do it in Canada. You go to the Permian.

The oil industry is not for the faint of heart. One day you're flush, the next you're staring down the possibility of a layoff. In a change we never saw coming, the operator who'd signed our deal was swept out in a mass firing, replaced overnight by men who didn't know us, didn't like us, and weren't interested in what we'd already delivered. Suddenly everything we had—our rigs, our contracts, our people—was stranded in the dust of West Texas. No contract. No way out. Our only hope was to convince the new leadership team to honor the contract, but negotiations aren't easy when the other side is refusing to yield any bit of its position. They told us we weren't good enough and accused us of not fulfilling the contract. We pointed out that we had lowered their costs, took their number of incidences to zero and massively increased efficiency, but none of it mattered. What we hoped would be a reasonable negotiation turned into an explosive argument. My partner's face was beet red, and our blood was boiling as hot as the 110-degree heat.

It didn't end in a deal. It ended in their head of security, a guy wearing a white cowboy hat and a revolver, who looked alarmingly like Clint Eastwood in Pale Rider, escorting us out of the building. I was sick to my stomach knowing that the next morning, I'd have to stand in front of our team—men who'd left their families and were counting on us—and tell them we were dead in the water. My voice cracked as I promised we'd find work because the truth was, I had no idea how I was going to keep that promise.

It took a few months, but eventually we rebuilt and even grew bigger. Looking back, I know where we went wrong and how we could have given ourselves a better chance at keeping that contract. We had gone in swinging when we should've gone in listening. That was before I understood tactical empathy, before I realized the real power in any negotiation is how well you understand the person on the other side of the table. It's making them feel heard when every instinct in your body is urging you to fight.

How might it have gone differently if instead of locking horns, we had listened? What if we'd focused less on proving we were right, and more on what they needed to hear? I hadn't read Chris Voss' book yet. But in hindsight that was the day I learned that sometimes you have to get escorted out at gunpoint to realize that in the oilfield, in Texas, in life—the biggest mistake you can make is thinking the loudest man in the room is the one in control.

UNDERSTAND WHAT MATTERS

My partner Jon and I worked well together and had fallen into a comfortable good-cop, bad-cop dynamic. He taught me how to be tough and stand my ground when the stakes were high, but

I learned that real power isn't in who can yell the loudest but in who can control the temperature in the room. Jon's way is to dig his heels in and go toe to toe. There's a time for that, especially in the Permian Basin where backbone is respected. But underneath that bravado are some universally human truths. People want to feel heard and understood. I'll never forget the deal that drove that lesson home.

We were closing in on a new client—big player that could change the trajectory of our business. We thought it was a slam dunk until the guy in charge said, "I don't think your rigs are heavy enough. We need bigger iron for this work." We knew damn well heavier rigs were overkill and would just cost more and slow things down. I could see that Jon was ready to go to battle. Instead, I repeated back what I heard—the concern behind the words, and said, "Sounds like what you're really worried about is that one job—that 10 percent—where a smaller rig might not cut it." He nodded. Bull's-eye! Then I laid out our experience, our track record, and said, "We'll have what you need if that day ever comes." After what felt like a ten-minute pause but was probably ten seconds he said, "All right. You've got the work."

That client stayed with us for years, and that bigger rig? It was never needed. There's a saying out here that everything's bigger in Texas, and it's true. There are big rigs, big money, big mouths, and big egos. But big doesn't always solve the problem. The tough oil executives won't be told what to do. The trick is to listen intently and affirm their words so perfectly that what you want becomes *their* idea. You don't walk in and tell a Texan how it's going to be. You prove you understand what matters to him. The ones who get that win the deals—and own the room.

It's All Your Fault

The oil field doesn't care how much you've invested, how new your equipment is, how much you miss your family up north or how hard you fought to get the contract. Out here, the minute something goes sideways, all eyes are on you, and you better be ready to handle it.

Coming out of the brutal 2016 downturn, when oil was scraping twenty-six dollars a barrel, we were hanging on by a thread. We'd just invested an additional five million dollars into brand-new equipment. After months of grinding, we finally had a shot—a full-year agreement on the table. All that was left was the final inspection.

The rig stood in a yard in Odessa, the work floor twenty-two feet in the air, staged for a full walk-through by the client's top brass. That's when the stairs gave out. Literally. As the tour wrapped and the executives made their way down, the metal stairs gave out beneath them. Two executives dropped nearly fifteen feet. One landed hard with his knees on the other man's back, both tangled in the twisted metal of the now demolished stairwell. We pulled them clear, got everyone to safety, and called for medical help. In that moment, I was pretty sure we had lost it all, so I wasn't surprised when the operations lead, a guy who always doubted us, looked at me with disdain and facetiously said, "Well, we'll let you know."

Just like that, months of work, five million dollars, and our shot at survival were on the line. What most people don't realize is that sometimes the best opportunity for success lies in the moments you think it's all over. Rather than throwing blame, we took full accountability. We didn't make excuses or shift blame to the welders or the manufacturers. We owned it. We acknowledged the severity of the problem and showed them exactly how we'd make it right.

The next week, we came back to the table with a plan that demonstrated our willingness to do whatever it took to make things right. We came prepared with a full Performance Improvement Plan. We didn't wait for them to tell us what was wrong. We laid it out—where we'd failed, why it happened, and exactly how we were going to fix it.

We didn't just promise change; we showed them the blueprint. That day, one rig went to the bench, but the others kept running and we turned that one rig agreement into a two-rig agreement with an option call for a third. Because when it mattered most, we took responsibility for the problem and gave them confidence in the solution. That's the part nobody teaches you about negotiating at the highest level. Owning the problem feels counterintuitive—as though admitting fault is giving up leverage. But it's the opposite. Accountability, when done right, is power. It earns trust. It calms the storm. In this business that's the difference between starting over and staying in the game.

Talking Isn't the Only Way to Negotiate

Looking back, I'd been learning to negotiate long before I ever sat at a boardroom table. I grew up playing rugby—a sport where strategy, timing, and control matter far more than brute strength. You don't just barrel through people, you read the field, anticipate your opponent and learn when to push and when to hold. You're negotiating the whole time without ever saying a word.

Business negotiations aren't much different. It's not about who talks loudest, it's about positioning. Creating openings. Timing your play so when you do speak, it lands how it should.

That lesson would hit me years later, when I left behind the safe corporate track to bet on the new company. I'd been working for a large rig company, interviewing for the national sales manager role—about as secure a job as you could get in that world. But I knew deep down, I was wired for entrepreneurship, and I was done playing safe. That's when I met Jon. He was starting a company—a one-rig boutique outfit—and he asked me to join. Two months later, the price of oil cratered. The whole Canadian market dried up overnight.

An old connection of Jon's told us to get to Texas where the action was. So we packed up and hauled our one rig across the border from Canada to Texas. I remember sitting alone in a two-bedroom apartment in Odessa, cold-calling giants like ExxonMobil—companies running a hundred rigs, just trying to get one shot. I made hundreds of calls and was repeatedly stonewalled by gatekeepers.

That's when it hit me—opportunity doesn't just start when you're in the room. It starts the moment they know who you are.

I hired a drone operator, shot footage of our rigs working, and loaded it all onto a handful of iPads, along with a handwritten note that said, "Give me a call—I'd love a chance to tell you more." Then I started dropping them off at the offices. Most of them ignored me but one night as I was standing in the kitchen making dinner with my wife, my phone rang. A completions manager from one of the major companies was on the other end. "I got your tablet," he said. "It's impressive. How do I get this thing back to you?" I told him I'd be in Houston the next week and would come pick it up myself. He laughed. "Good. You can do your pitch then."

That tablet got me through more gatekeepers than a thousand cold calls ever could. That's the part most people miss—negotiation isn't just about talking. Sometimes, whether it's rugby, rigs, or million-dollar contracts—the win doesn't go to the loudest guy. It goes to the one who knows when to stop talking about how great they are—and starts *showing* it.

What Matters More Than the Millions

We built this business with three of us—me, Jon, and John. Three guys chasing opportunity in an unforgiving industry where absolutely nothing is guaranteed. We handled every part of the operation ourselves, built it from the ground up, and clawed our way into a respected place in the Permian Basin.

We've won contracts. We've won awards. We lost contracts, employees, and pride, and had to rebuild. It's a roller coaster of unexpected change, but the thread that remains consistent is this: At the end of the day it's all powered by people. The people are what matters.

John—the VP and a cofounder of our business—died in his sleep at just sixty-five years old. Weeks later another close and much younger friend died suddenly from a gallstone incident, leaving behind two young children. And then, as I flew in the morning of my friend's funeral, I got the call that my father-in-law—the man who'd filled the role of father since I lost my own back in 2002—was in the hospital. Cancer. A month later he was gone too.

That year was a reckoning—a cold reminder that time doesn't care how hard you're working or how big your company gets. None of it matters as much as the relationships we build and the integrity we demonstrate. What matters is our willingness to put our own egos aside and truly aim to connect to and understand the people around us. I used to be a huge worrier until a friend told me, "If you worry about something that hasn't happened yet, you're worrying about nothing – something that currently doesn't exist." And he was right. All that energy wasted on what *might* go wrong—when the only thing that matters is what you're building right now, in this moment. It forced me to ask the question most men spend their whole lives avoiding: What am I really leaving behind?

This business is not just about rigs, pipe, and iron. It's about the people. It's about the way you carry yourself when the stakes are high and nothing is certain. What I know now is that whether I'm in the oil field in Texas or sitting with my family at dinner, my presence, empathy, and genuine desire to learn more are always required. Ultimately, my word, character, and reputation are the only currency that matters. I don't need to be the loudest guy in the room or the biggest name on the wellhead. I want to be the one they remember when the dust finally settles—the guy who stayed in the saddle, rode out every storm, and kept his word. In this industry, you learn fast—it's not the man who charges through the gate that wins. It's the one who takes time to assess the situation. It's the one who over-prepares and learns to intuit what's *not* being said. Everything might be bigger in Texas, but it's not the size of your iron or the volume of your voice that keeps you in the game. It's the grit to stand your ground, the humility to listen, and the wisdom to know which one the moment calls for.

About Marc

Marc Rampaul entered the oil industry after obtaining a Bachelor of Commerce (honors) with a double major in international business and marketing.

With over twenty years of experience in drilling and completions and a certification in production accounting, Marc has demonstrated a consistent ability to drive strategic initiatives, lead cross-functional teams, and achieve substantial revenue growth. His expertise encompasses market analysis and client performance management systems, working closely with the operator and the service provider's teams to develop high-performing team dynamics across various divisions and service lines.

Marc has a passion for bringing innovative solutions to market. In 2013 he started Patch Innovations Inc., an oil and gas consulting firm designed to aid in the effort to bring new oil field technologies and turnkey packages to market.

Patch has extensive experience developing new innovative solutions and combining multiple service lines to create competitive advantages through increased safety and efficiency. Patch is committed to achieving operational excellence by building long-term partnerships focused on monitoring and reporting operational efficiencies, increased safety, and quality assurance.

Since 2014 Marc has played a pivotal role in growing a small well servicing company from its inception to a thriving enterprise in the Permian Basin. He cultivated a collaborative culture and guided his teams toward shared objectives that reflect core values, thereby achieving substantial organic growth.

In his leisure time Marc enjoys traveling with his wife and three children. The family maintains an active lifestyle through various sports, including hockey, rugby, ringette, golf, and skiing, participating in these activities as players, coaches, or spectators.

Marc is committed to continual improvement in both his personal and professional life, consistently engaging with literature, audio, and visual media focused on personal development.

CHAPTER 14

FOOD (AND BEVERAGE) FOR THOUGHT

By Gary Steininger

I stared down at my phone, stunned as the media delivered mind-boggling and unprecedented headlines: "Federal Leaders Order Historic Lockdown to Fight Virus Outbreak." "Shelter in Place Mandates Amid Growing Coronavirus Fears."

Suddenly the phone started ringing—and for hours never stopped. Panic was pouring in from every direction. Busboys, servers, bartenders, managers—people I'd worked shoulder to shoulder with—terrified at the prospect of the restaurant shutting down. And I got it. After more than thirty years running, revitalizing, and modernizing food and beverage operations—from mom-and-pop eateries to PGA-level country clubs and large-scale casino operations—I knew exactly what was at stake. "How are we going to make it?" they asked. "Will we even have jobs next week?"

Like a lot of people, I'd spent most of my career chasing the next rung on the ladder. I had been sitting in a leadership seat for a long time at that point, but that day, I realized that my role now extended beyond management and operations. My team was spiraling, time-traveling into the worst possible outcomes, putting all their energy into what *might* happen instead of what they could control. What they needed was for me to be the calm, consistent presence as we navigated completely uncharted waters. I needed to acknowledge their fear without feeding it. This was a moment I'd trained for—not just in a business setting but in hours spent sitting in meditation and practicing martial arts. Years of learning how to sit still with uncertainty, stare it down, and not flinching were being called to the mat. So I listened. I let them unload every worst-case scenario and piece by piece walked them back from the edge.

I gave them what they really needed—*presence*. "We don't need to worry yet. All we need to do is handle what's right in front of us. Together. Let's talk about what we can do *now.*"

When you change the conversation, you change the energy. You shift the focus from fear to possibility. You stop asking, "What if everything goes wrong," and start asking, "What if we get through this better than we were before?"

And we did. We opened back up and were busier than ever. When you lead with empathy, you provide a sense of safety, and in that energy, solutions can form. What I learned in that moment has stayed with me ever since—empathy isn't soft. It's the sharpest tool you have. It creates connection and builds trust. Most of all, it gives people the confidence to quiet their fears and assumptions and move forward with *hope*.

THE PATIENCE GAME

Leadership, just like martial arts, isn't about reacting with brute force—it's about flipping the script, staying calm under pressure, and practicing small, precise skills every day until they're automatic. It's muscle memory. You train not for the easy moments but for the crisis—the moment you don't see coming.

That's why martial arts and leadership are the same game. People think of martial arts as tough, aggressive fighting, but anyone who's spent real time on the mat knows it's a game of patience and precision. You don't overpower; you outlast, outthink, outflow. Every move is small but intentional, designed to create the advantage without ever breaking a sweat.

The origins of it all—tai chi—are proof of that. Most people don't realize that tai chi was the original martial art, and everything else—karate, judo, aikido—came from it. And what's the hallmark of tai chi? It's slow. Deliberate. *Self-controlled.* The same applies to leadership. You build the habits *before* the pressure cooker hits.

When COVID blindsided us, I saw firsthand what happens when people don't have that training. Simple problems turned into complex nightmares because so many people didn't know how to sit in discomfort. To become curious. They hadn't built the muscle.

And honestly, most of the leaders in this business haven't either. At fifty-five I'm still one of the *younger* leaders left running formal food and beverage operations. Most of the people still managing grew up leading in the '70s, '80s, and '90s—or were trained by those who did. Their technical knowledge is invaluable, no doubt. But their methods? Outdated. Their people skills? Declining.

I see the scorn in their eyes every time I lean in to empathy. They think I'm wasting time. That I'm soft. But what they don't see is that tactical empathy is how you turn a nervous, unsure employee into a loyal, empowered contributor. I've used Black Swan methods for years to transform chaotic, dysfunctional operations into smooth, reputable, high-performing teams. I've rebuilt operations where guest satisfaction soars, sales increase, profits grow, morale improves, and employee retention hits 90 percent—in an industry where 90 percent turnover is considered normal.

And yet they still resist, because it takes time and patience. It's Socratic leadership. You guide. You ask. You create space for people to find their own answers. It's like planting a tree in fertile soil instead of screaming at it to grow. But when leadership still runs on "my way or the highway," they lose people before they ever have a chance to grow. You see it in old-school chefs running kitchens like military camps—where every road leads back to the guy in the tallest white hat. You see it in service managers treating staff like cogs in a machine—replaceable, disposable. There's no empathy. No connection. No explanation of *why* someone should give more than the bare minimum.

And that's the difference. Real leadership doesn't come from authority; it comes from the ability to show people *why* they should care. And after all these years, if there's one thing I know about this industry, it's this: Hospitality runs a hell of a lot better when the only thing getting thrown around the kitchen is a plate of pasta, not someone's dignity.

SOFT TACTICS FOR HARDHEADS

I heard the clang of dishes rattling as the guy's fist slammed on the table.

Four guys were sitting at a table in the restaurant and had already enjoyed a few rounds of alcohol. Dinner was set in front of them, and suddenly the leader of the pack screamed at the server, "Why would you disrespect me like this? Why are you trying to ruin our evening?" He was shouting profanities, and all the other patrons had set their forks down to stare. There was no time to plan, but luckily the years of martial-arts training kicked in, and I walked calmly over to the table, unbothered by the red face and flared nostrils in front of me. It was clear to me what needed to happen. This guy had an ego, and it needed a stroke. I adopted my best late-night FM DJ voice and labeled his feelings. "Clearly, this wasn't what you were expecting," I said. "It looks like we made a mistake." I took the hit. No defensiveness. Just ownership. Then I leaned in and said, "I get it. You're here with your buddies, having a good time, expecting a giant steak. That's what tonight was supposed to be about, right?" "Yeah, that's right," he grunted. Bingo. Once he said those words, I knew I could take him from a ten to a two! "Would you be opposed to waiting a few minutes?" I asked. "I'll get you the nicest steak in the city. No questions asked."

And just like that, his posture softened. He apologized, not just to me but to his friends and even to the surrounding tables.

What set him off was silly. He wanted a steak *bigger* than what we had on the menu. That was it. But it was never about the steak. It was about being seen, heard, and respected—even in the middle of his most obnoxious moment. And that's what tactical empathy looks like. No ego. No emotion. Just resolution. In my younger days I would've fired right back. I would've matched his energy, maybe told him where he could stick that steak. But that's not leadership; that's ego, and my goal was not to win but to defuse the situation.

The first rule of leadership is simple: Don't escalate—even when they deserve it. *Especially* when they deserve it. Instead of joining their chaos, lend them your calm. Tactical empathy is martial arts for the mind—controlled, disciplined, and powerfully effective. If you can stay curious, stay calm, and stay in control when someone's at their worst—you both win. Every time.

GET ACCOUNTABLE OR GET BURNED!

What most people call problems, I've learned to see as opportunities. What I've found is that sometimes the most loyal customers weren't a result of perfect service but of a disaster handled properly. That's where tactical empathy becomes a strategy, not just a feel-good buzzword. I'll never forget the afternoon one of my servers made a rookie mistake and set a coffee pitcher on the ledge behind a guest. Next thing you know, the whole pot comes down— scalding hot coffee poured straight down the man's back. We had to call an ambulance, and he suffered second-degree burns.

In moments like that we have two choices: defend or dive in. It's human nature to try to put distance between yourself and the disaster with phrases such as, "It wasn't my fault." But I knew that this was not a matter of fault but of accountability. I preemptively covered the customer's medical expenses and then—because it was the right thing to do—we brought lunch to the hospital waiting room, not for show, but because empathy means demonstrating that you genuinely care!

That one move shifted everything. Instead of a lawsuit, we built loyalty. After he recovered, that man and his family became some of our most regular brunch guests. Week after week they came back because what could have destroyed trust became the thing that built it.

And here's the thing: None of that happens if your priority is being *right*. Most people get stuck there. "It wasn't my fault," they say. "Why should I take the blame?" But you've got two choices in that moment: you can be right, or you can accomplish your goal. Reagan said it best: "There is no limit to what a man can do or where he can go if he doesn't mind who gets the credit." And I'll expand on that: There's no limit to what you can achieve if instead of running *from* responsibility, you run *toward* it!

HIGH STAKES AND HOT DOGS

It's easy to think tactical empathy is just a tool for business negotiations, hostage situations, or high-stakes deals, but it's actually a way of moving through the world. It's a skill set that extends far beyond the workplace, allowing you to defuse tension, connect with people, and demonstrate compassion and diplomacy in your everyday life.

I've got a happy-go-lucky Lab-Dane mix that likes to go to the dog park. One Saturday, as my dog ran around without a care in the world, I heard a commotion brewing. A young man dressed in what I can only describe as antisocial armor, stood with his German shepherd. His dog wasn't just aggressive. He was unmistakably predatory. Several people grabbed their little dogs and made a beeline for the exit. Call me stubborn, but it was a nice day, and I wasn't going anywhere. I walked up and offered my hand. "Gary," I said. He stared and defensively replied, "So what." Now, after years of training, I know that if someone's reaction to a simple statement is coming in hot at a nine out of ten, something else is going on. If your spouse flips out about the toothpaste in the sink, you can bet they aren't talking about toothpaste. I dropped my volume. "Are you OK?" He fired back, "Dogs need to learn not to be dominated." That told me he knew what his dog was doing. But *his* aggression? That was a shield. Then came the one line that told me everything: "You have to stand up for yourself, or others will beat you down."

I leaned in. "You're going to think I'm a real jerk for asking this—you might even want to swing at me. But are we talking about the dog right now, or are we talking about you?"

That broke it wide open. Turned out his whole life had been a fight. He had been physically abused by his father and had learned that strength meant intimidation. I listened and ultimately connected him with a therapist and a dog trainer I trust.

You see, tactical empathy isn't just for high stakes negotiations and rowdy customers. It's a way of seeing people—the pain behind the armor, the story behind the cutting tone. It's how you turn potential enemies into friends and make the world a little gentler one conversation at a time. I haven't seen him back at the dog park, but I've got high hopes both for him and his four-legged friend.

THE LONG GAME IS THE ONLY GAME

Statistically, food and beverage management ranks as the second-most-stressful job behind air-traffic control. The average guest barely acknowledges the server as a human. Often, hardworking people doing their best so they can support their families are treated at best like background noise and at worst like gum on the bottom of a shoe! Orders are barked at them. Complaints land on them, and yet the best of them stays calm and creates solutions. Anyone can win *once* by swinging harder or yelling louder, but in the restaurant we're not playing for the check in front of you. We're playing for the return visit and the referrals. Getting them to trust you so they come back is where the real win is.

That angry guest, that burned customer, or whoever it may be doesn't remember what you said. They remember how you made them feel. And they remember who stayed calm when everything around them was on fire and who treated them kindly when they didn't deserve it.

Empathy isn't soft; it's strategic. It's how you flip the script without raising your voice. It's how you turn "one-and-done" transactions into lasting and profitable relationships. But here's the Jedi-level move—the thing that changes *everything* about how you show up: Decide ahead of time that you like the person. Mean it if you can, because once you choose to like the other person, you stop defending yourself and start leaning in. You stop trying to win and start listening. You halt your assumptions and get genuinely curious.

That's leadership. Slow it down. Play the long game, because the ones who come out on top aren't the loudest—they're the calmest. And once you learn to play that way, you don't just win the moment; you win the whole game.

About Gary

"You are the integration of your passions and the combined knowledge of everyone who came before you." This powerful phrase has guided Gary Steininger throughout decades of success in the food and beverage industry. For Gary, it reflects the profound impact of others' devotion to our growth, a principle he now dedicates his career to passing on for the benefit of others.

Gary has spent over thirty years opening, revitalizing, and modernizing a wide range of food and beverage operations. From mom-and-pop eateries to PGA-level country clubs and large-scale casino operations, he has a hard-won title of "the fixer." Gary has identified a few simple universal principles to success for anyone in hospitality. He currently trains staff to meet today's market demands while inspiring them to see a bigger picture. His expertise spans every facet of the industry, honed through hands-on experience and a commitment to operational excellence.

Gary's journey began with a foundational education in accounting at the University of Nevada, Las Vegas, where he gained critical insights into the financial sustainability and efficiency of hotel and hospitality businesses. He furthered his education by learning directly from industry leaders, great chefs, entrepreneurs, servers, and dishwashers—all who taught him the art and science of food and beverage operations. Though he's rooted in Nevada, Gary's approach to mentorship and growth has been applied nationwide, reflecting his belief that fostering people, sales, and profits is not just a skill but a duty to share.

Based in Reno, Gary balances his professional endeavors with a rich personal life. He continues to serve as a high school golf coach, a tai chi instructor, and a devoted husband to his wife, Christina, and father to their son, Aiden, and their Labra-Dane dog, Magnolia.

Contact him at Fullglassedge.com or on X at fullglassedge.

CHAPTER 15

NEGOTIATION MINDSET

By John O'Farrell

He was two hundred kilos of Yugoslavian fury. They called him the Godfather.

I met him when my twin brother, who had gone to the UK to work in the hospitality industry, contracted pneumonia and ended up in intensive care. My mother and I immediately hopped on a plane and were picked up in a sleek Jaguar, chauffeur driven, courtesy of the Godfather himself.

A former business owner turned hotel tycoon, he owned three hotels, including the nineteenth-century-style French château we were staying in—two hundred acres of fairy-tale countryside and old-world wealth. He was six-foot-five, was built like a brick house, and ran his hotels with an iron fist. My brother was working for him when he got sick, and he felt responsible. He sat with me and my mother every night, and after a few days we had built a great rapport. Once my brother recovered, it was time for us to go home to Ireland. That's when the Godfather said, "How would you feel about staying on for a hotel management program here?"

I was eighteen and hadn't even considered a career in hospitality, but when you're enjoying five-star treatment and have built a rapport with the man everyone else feared, it's an offer that's tough to pass on, so I accepted. In my first year, he fired me *twice, wrongly,* before I earned his respect. One minute I was training a new girl in the restaurant; the next, he was throwing things in the kitchen because she'd made a mistake while I covered another department. She messed up. I paid for it. He berated me with a string of expletives, yelling at me, "Go back to Ireland," but I didn't flinch. I stood there, defiantly facing this giant of a man, and said, "No problem." I knew I had done nothing wrong and wasn't going to cower. The next morning, he called me. "Why aren't you here? Your shift is starting." Fifteen minutes later I was back on shift. That night, he apologized to me in front of everyone. The executive chef leaned and said, "I've never seen him apologize to anyone. He respects you. There's something there." And there was.

I didn't know it at the time, but that moment became the foundation of my career. You see, he didn't just teach me how to survive a five-star hotel floor. He taught me how to read people as though I was learning a new language. One day he made me sit in the lobby with him for hours. Just sitting and watching. While my colleagues rushed around serving guests, he mentored me. "You see that businessman in the suit?" he said. "He's a wolf. And I'll tell you why. That woman over there—she's a lamb. And that one? A fox." It sounded ridiculous to me at first—until it didn't. He was teaching me behavioral pattern recognition. He was training me to profile emotions before interaction. He was giving me a *system*.

What I saw was empathy in its rawest, most powerful form. Empathy is often mistaken as a synonym for sympathy, a natural inclination to feel for someone else. A "soft" skill. But to put empathy in that box dilutes its strategic power. I didn't realize it or call it this at the time, but I know now that what we were practicing was *precision empathy*. It's tactical. Strategic. *Useful*. It's the kind that makes people feel seen, valued, and understood and is a bridge to resolving conflict, soothing nerves, and closing contracts. Within eighteen months of being at the château, I was managing entire events—unheard of at that age. But I had learned to *read* people. To understand the story behind the suit, the fear behind the anger, and the trigger behind the complaint. I was beginning to understand how to read a situation but also read the people *in* the situation.

Empathy gave me the edge, not because it made me nicer but because it made me *more aware*. With his mentorship I learned that the greatest advantage in any negotiation, any business, any room is the ability to read the people in it.

My Number One Skill

I've spent thirty-five years in the hospitality industry. I started tough. I got things done, and didn't have time to play nice doing it. After all, I learned from the Godfather! After leaving the château, I spent eight years at sea as Chief Purser on passenger ships. Conflict management training was a standard part of the job. It must be when you're floating across the Irish Sea with a few thousand passengers. We were trained to deal with all eventualities: intoxication, medical emergencies, and even how to evacuate thousands of passengers in a limited amount of time. I built a reputation fast, but I'm not sure it was a good one. One day a mentor of mine told me, "When you board a ship, people run for cover. You've got presence," he said. "But if you don't soften that edge, it's going to work against you." I was confident, maybe a little arrogant. I knew my stuff, and people were afraid to challenge me. That might sound like a good position to be in as a leader, but it's not. If no one talks to you, you're not learning anything. I had to rewire something big in my leadership style. That realization didn't come overnight.

At thirty-five, I was headhunted to run the largest hotel operation in Ireland. Turns out it wasn't *one* hotel—it was four. A twelve-hundred-bedroom property, a PGA golf course, a wedding venue, and a private airport. Overnight I was managing thousands of rooms, major events, and negotiating international contracts, UEFA, Disney, and events with the Dalai Lama. It was high-stakes, and I thought being tough would gain respect. But negotiations weren't landing the way they used to, and I was frustrated. I made up my mind to study negotiations at Harvard Law School, among other global institutions.

I learned to master the art of negotiations and strategic communication and quickly learned that tactical empathy was vital to success. I also discovered the strategic approach to active listening; there's a difference between listening and hearing. Listening for what's been said, and more importantly what's not been said. The definition of *hearing* is to perceive sounds. Listening, on the other hand, garners information. It was also important for me to be curious about the other side's motives, fears, and desires. My focus now went from *What's in it for me?* to *What's in it for them?* Things started to shift. People began to open up, and deals were easier to make. It's not that I lost my edge—I sharpened a new one.

Tactical empathy became my number one skill. At first, it felt counterintuitive, slowing down, and opening up. But now? I realize it's the most powerful move on the table. Because empathy, when used with precision, doesn't just connect—it *influences*. Since leaning back in to empathy, I've built tremendously loyal teams that are loyal not out of fear but out of respect. I started to master negotiations and learned that we spend most of our day negotiating whether we realize it or not. It's not a skill reserved for boardrooms and contract disputes. Even a casual conversation with a passenger or guest is a negotiation. And in an industry that is known for its fast pace and ticking time bombs, it helps to know that *every conflict is a negotiation yet to happen.*

Defusing the Bombs

One of the most challenging conversations I've ever faced was with an aggressive guest aboard a ship. I was Chief Purser at the time and received a call about a serious incident on the top deck. He had injured his partner physically, and was in a highly emotional state and under the influence.

As I approached the scene, my priority was the safety of the guests and the injured party. I knew better than to rush in. I reached the deck and saw him—agitated and damaging the ship's interior with his fists. He turned on me, screaming, mistaking me for the police because of my naval uniform. I slowly removed my jacket and epaulettes, small moves that made a big difference. This was a small fire that without intervention could become a raging inferno!

I spoke with confidence and asked open-ended questions. I gave him my name and asked for his, but he didn't reply. I noticed a football club tattoo on his arm and made a comment about the team's striker. I got a brief flicker of connection, then more rage.

I calmly persuaded him to allow his partner to be escorted away. That gave us privacy. No audience. No pressure. Just him and me. I calmed him down, and he later shared that he'd just lost a family member and didn't know how to cope. I asked to sit. Asking permission was important. I didn't judge or give advice. I listened. I steered the conversation with care, reframing questions that helped him feel heard and in control. That's when he finally gave me his name. Once we had established trust, the incident began to deescalate. I also knew I had to have a plan if he lost control and physically attacked me as he did his partner. I didn't treat him like an aggressor; I treated him as a person suffering. That was the key. That, and a little neuroscience! You see, when someone is in a highly emotional state, they are operating from the right side of their brain. By asking questions about his tattoo, I switched on the left side of the brain, steering him away from his intense emotions, if just for a moment.

In my experience, when emotion takes over, people struggle to override their fears. They focus on the consequence of their actions. When we meet volatility with humanity—when we listen instead of lecture, connect instead of control—we disarm chaos. In high-stakes situations, treating someone as a person rather than a problem doesn't just de-escalate the moment; it can transform it.

WINNING WITH INTEGRITY

Throughout my career, negotiations have always been an integral part of my success. Empathy became one of my greatest tools. One of my earliest negotiations put everything I'd learned to the test. This particular negotiation was complex. I was involved in a high-stakes negotiation as a consultant, which involved a long, bitter history between two firms. I knew we were up against a formidable opponent and reputations were on the line, including my own. As the negotiation approached, their team maintained a bullish posture, and there was a rumor that they'd already booked a venue for their victory celebration.

On the morning of the negotiation, our team arrived at a mutual location, but the other side didn't show. We learned they'd changed the venue at the last minute to throw us off. We were now forced to negotiate on their turf, at their head office. Even numbers at the table had been agreed upon, but when we entered the boardroom, they had doubled their number of people to add to the intimidation. Amid all the confusion, I received a text from my office: "Don't start the negotiation without calling in. We've got these guys." I excused myself, made the call, and what I learned changed everything.

Turns out we had uncovered an old and binding agreement that completely undercut their position. If revealed publicly, it would cause enormous humiliation for their leadership team and in particular the owner of the firm. My employer bellowed, "Go for the jugular." But I had a different plan. I returned to the boardroom, walked up to the owner of their firm, and quietly requested a private conversation outside. Once outside, I calmly laid out what we'd found. I watched his face shift—confusion, panic, realization. He knew the cards had flipped. We had every advantage. And yet I chose not to expose him publicly. I told him plainly, "There's no value for me in destroying your reputation." He was stunned. It took him a moment to grasp what I was saying, and he was grateful that I had spared him the embarrassment of public exposure. The major conflict was resolved. But what came next was unexpected—referrals, introductions, and recommendations from his firm for years to come. That day, empathy was my most powerful ally.

By protecting his dignity, I built long-term credibility and created a win-win outcome. I passed on the ego trip and chose integrity.

The reality is that most negotiations involve trying to take something, ask for something, or defend a position—which means the other side must give in or give something up. Now add an array of emotions into the mix—fear, pride, pressure—and you'll see that logic alone won't close the deal. Empathy can bridge that gap.

The Legacy Lives On

If there's one thing I've learned across decades in hospitality, highstakes negotiations, and leadership, it's this: Empathy isn't weakness. It's intelligence, wielded wisely. The world seems to glorify louder voices and harder lines, yet sometimes saying nothing has more power and influence in hostile situations. Empathize with your counterpart; look for the opportunity to engage on a different, more meaningful level.

The Godfather didn't just teach me to run hotels; he taught me to read people. To sit in silence and watch. To notice. To listen. That skill has taken me further than any title ever could.

Years later I brought my son to meet him. We'd kept in touch all that time, and I wanted him to see where it all began and meet the man who saw something in me before I saw it in myself. Watching my son engage with him, I realized this wasn't just mentorship. It was a legacy. I was carrying forward a legacy of leadership.

Whether I was facing a furious passenger at sea or a rival across the boardroom table, the outcome hinged on the same principle: People yearn for recognition, Underneath the chaos, there's always a story waiting to be told. I've sat across from grief. From fear. From ego. And time and again, empathy has been the key that unlocks resolution, respect, and results. I've been the one with all the answers. I've also been the one who got it wrong. And what I know now is this: What separates good leaders from great ones isn't how intimidating they are; it's how well they listen to what's being said and their ability to recognize hidden potential.

That's the legacy I carry forward—not just from the Godfather but from every conversation, every conflict, every moment where

I choose connection over control, because in the end the greatest negotiator isn't the one who wins the argument; it's the one who transforms the room and every person in it. And that's the kind of legacy worth leaving.

About John

John O'Farrell is a distinguished figure in the realms of hospitality and negotiations, boasting over thirty years of extensive industry experience. As the managing director of a leading IoT supply company, he has established himself as a pivotal player in the tech supply industry, leveraging his deep knowledge and expertise to drive innovation and foster strategic partnerships.

John's academic credentials are as impressive as his professional achievements. He honed his skills in negotiations by studying at Harvard Law and Business Schools, gaining invaluable insights into the intricacies of international dealmaking. His education has equipped him with a comprehensive understanding of legal and business frameworks, which he applies adeptly in his current role.

Before transitioning into the tech supply industry, John played a crucial role in managing some of the largest hotel operations in Ireland. His extensive background in hospitality has not only enriched his understanding of the sector but also provided him with the experience necessary to navigate complex operational challenges. As a skilled asset manager, he was responsible for negotiating intricate transactions on behalf of multiple global clients, demonstrating his ability to balance diverse interests while achieving optimal outcomes.

John's training in diplomacy across the European Union has further enhanced his negotiation skills. He possesses a unique aptitude for understanding different cultural perspectives and leveraging them to create win-win situations. This skill set has proved invaluable, especially in a globalized business environment where cross-border negotiations are commonplace.

In addition to his professional endeavours, John is passionate about mentoring the next generation of leaders in the events and hospitality industry. He actively supports large-scale operators, sharing his wealth of knowledge and experience to help them navigate the complexities of their businesses. His commitment to mentorship reflects his belief in the importance of fostering talent and encouraging innovation within the industry.

John O'Farrell's dedication to excellence in hospitality and negotiations, combined with his extensive experience and educational background, positions him as a leading authority in his field. He continues to shape the industry landscape through his work, inspiring others to strive for success and embrace the opportunities presented by an ever-evolving market.

CHAPTER 16

BREAKFAST IN JAIL

*The Moment That Flipped My Script
and Changed My Life*

By Jason "JT" Thomas

"**H**ere's your breakfast, bitch."

The guard threw the tray with disgusting food through the bars, and it landed with a thud, sending half of it onto the dirty floor. That was the moment. Rock bottom. I sat on that metal bed, staring at the mess on the floor, and wondered, "How did I get here?" How did a kid with so much promise, good parents, and big dreams end up in a jail cell?

The thing is, you don't just wake up one day as a criminal. It's not one decision. It's a hundred small and misguided ones. I wasn't born a jerk—heck, I was a Boy Scout—but that didn't stop me from becoming one. Until I was thirty, I had a take-no-prisoners attitude and would've run over anyone in my way. I had no empathy. I didn't see people as people—only as tools or threats. Empathy? That was a word for suckers. I didn't give a damn about what you were feeling. I only cared if you were standing in my way. And when you live like that, the universe eventually throws you into a jail cell and says, "Now are you ready to listen?" I learned that the hard way.

I grew up in what I call *low* middle America. My parents were always loving and did everything they could to give my brother and me what we wanted, but money often ran short, and that reality never sat right with me. So at eight years old I was already mowing lawns. Collecting those dollar bills and tucking them away flipped a switch in me that only heightened my hunger for more. At some point, it became clear that my mental health was tied directly to my bank account. I didn't want to just survive. I wanted to thrive—so much so that as soon as I was legally able to, I started skating to a produce stand at 5 a.m. to earn my first real paycheck. But it wouldn't be long before I found out there were things I could sell that would go for a hell of a lot more money than apples.

THE FIRST SCRIPT

We all have a script we inherit. Mine looked normal from the outside. I had *Leave It to Beaver* parents who stayed married and in love until my mom passed. My parents did their best to hide any struggles, and they did well. It wasn't until I was an adult and could look back at it that I saw how tight money was and that they did their best to shield me from any of life's harsh realities. Eventually, I internalized this message: If you want peace, security, control, you need money. Period. But there's a dangerous side to that mindset. When your worth is tied to your wallet, you don't just hustle; you hustle *at all costs*. That's how the script flips in the wrong direction. And usually we don't notice that the train is off the rails until it's running us over.

The need for fast cash led me to the restaurant world and its promise of fast cash and big tips. I loved it, and as a fifteen-year-old schoolkid, I was making enough money that I would lose a few hundred dollars every month, only to find it when I eventually cleaned my room, and my mom still had to fight me to do so. That's where I met the drug scene. It was just another hustle. Drugs weren't about rebellion for me; they were about efficiency, but I did have my share of fun too. I was an entrepreneurial-minded kid, so selling came naturally to me, and there seemed to be no shortage of customers looking to party. By fifteen I was arrested for selling LSD in class. Unbeknownst to me at the time, it happened to be fake, but the cop who arrested me didn't care, and the charges weren't all that different. I got expelled and, after a few weeks incarcerated, spent my sophomore year at a reform school for screwups. That should've been a wake-up call. It wasn't. It was more like a master-class to getting better at the hustle.

When I got back to school for my junior year, I became the guy everyone envied. I was popular, I always had cash, and the proverbial hot new girl who just moved to town took a liking to me. The runaway train kept going, and after lots of parties and very little schoolwork, I never had a senior year—because I had a daughter instead. I was determined to provide for her, so I dropped out of school to work and save money. Now, that might sound noble, but here's the thing: Doing the right thing with the wrong mindset can still wreck your life. A month before the baby was born, I got a cryptic message from a friend: "You should go over there," it said. I did. And there was my fiancé on the porch looking very cozy with another guy.

Eight months pregnant and cheating on me. Needless to say, we didn't part on good terms. I was pushed out of my daughter's early life. And that, mixed with the heartache of losing my first love in that way, shaped everything that came next.

Sometimes we *think* we're flipping the script. We *say* we want change. But really we're just finding a new backdrop for the same story. I made sure that child support was paid every month, but it wasn't enough, and landscaping wasn't going to cut it. Eventually, I reverted to selling drugs until a deal gone wrong with the Arab mafia forced me to leave town. I got my GED, forged some paperwork, and joined the Navy. Sounds like a redemption arc, right? Wrong.

Six months later I was discharged for a failed drug test—caused, ironically, by a *legal* supplement. That crushed me. I finally thought I was doing it right and still got slammed. That's when I realized, if you don't actually change your inner script, you'll keep attracting the same chaos, even when your behavior looks different.

There I was, back in Orlando, with no job prospects and no direction. Hope wasn't going to pay the bills, but selling weed would. One day I met my daughter's mother at the local Wally

World so that I could follow her back to her aunt's house for the rare opportunity to see my daughter. She asked if she could smoke with me, and I had a little in my truck, so I said sure, why not. In my young and dumb mind, I thought we might be turning a page and could try to be friends. It was a setup. Her boyfriend, who was a police officer, was waiting. That was how I ended up busted, cuffed, and thrown in jail for the second time. And that morning, in a dank prison cell as my breakfast tray hit the floor, *I was finally pissed off enough at myself to make the changes necessary to break the cycle.* I saw the path ahead. Death. Prison. A life wasted. And for the first time in years I felt a fire light inside me. Not one lit by greed. This was a fire lit by purpose.

TAKING THE PEN

When I was released from jail, I was determined to rewrite the direction of my story. I did my probation while living back with my parents as a much different and finally humbled man. The only thing I knew how to do *legally* was hospitality. So I worked my way up. Shift by shift. There would be no more shortcuts, and I worked my ass off, climbing my way up to a coveted management position. It worked for a while, until one night I looked around me. I still wasn't going anywhere, and the prospect of being behind the bar as a fifty-year-old man, slinging drinks as if he were still twenty-five, was something that terrified me. I didn't want to die behind a bar. I had big goals and a much more expansive vision for my life, and it wasn't going to happen doing shift work in the service industry, no matter what the title was.

I had to take a breath and think about the trajectory of my life. I had to zero in on what I was good at and what had always made me happy. The answer was fitness. I had always been an athlete, so the most logical move was to become a personal trainer. Eventually, I was working with pro MMA fighters and running a team of trainers in my first somewhat successful business endeavor. For once I wasn't just surviving—I was *building* something. Here's where empathy starts to creep in—not as a tactic but as a *mirror*. I was coaching fighters. High performers. Big egos. And I started to see something in them I hadn't seen in myself before: pain, vulnerability, self-doubt.

I began listening more and talking less. I started realizing that people weren't lazy; they were afraid. People didn't quit on goals because they didn't care but because they cared too much. The fear of failure was enough to make them walk away from even the most well-planned path. I had to learn how to navigate those emotional roller coasters with my clients. The better I got at making them feel seen, the more successful they were. I was strengthening my empathy muscle client by client and realizing that it wasn't a weakness. It was the sharpest tool in my toolbox. It lets you decode people's motives. It helps to de-escalate conflict. And it helps you make an impact, allowing me to form deep connections in a way manipulation never could.

Eventually, the long hours and big egos that came with training high-profile athletes led me straight to burnout. Paddleboarding was booming at the time, and I happened to meet the guy who ran the largest paddleboarding company in Florida. He offered me a job, and I became the stunt guy. After I had worked with them for a little while and learned the ropes, my mom, who was a tax consultant and had tons of connections in the tourism industry, said, "Bring paddleboarding to the Disney area. It'll blow up!" I took the idea to my boss, and instead of praising my enterprising spirit, he got angry. Not only did he not want to partner, but he told me to take a hike in not-so-pleasant words. I wasn't going to let that stop me, so I launched my own paddleboard company. Unfortunately, Central Florida weather made business tough *and* my plan for consistent income nearly impossible.

So I flipped again—bubble soccer. A viral video of Jimmy Fallon playing with giant inflatable balls sparked an idea. I bought a set of them and started renting them out. It did so well that before long I was the national sales director of Knockerball USA, helping scale the company to 150 affiliates and over one million dollars in revenue in the first year alone. Then another train derailment. I heard about an archery product that I knew in my gut would be a great complement to our business, so I started a new venture. I meant for it to be a *part* of our company, but my boss saw it as an adversarial move and fired me five days before Christmas. Bummer.

I went solo. I built my own product line, dealt with manufacturing in China, and navigated slander videos and legal threats from competitors, but I wasn't giving up. I would keep flipping my script until my story unfolded exactly as I wanted it to. Each change wasn't just survival; it was strategy. And it worked. I did well in that business, but I eventually closed the doors after trade with China became increasingly more difficult. That gave me the opportunity to return to what I always loved: training and coaching—only this time my clients wouldn't be athletes but business owners, mainly entrepreneurs who owned gyms and water-sports companies. It was a great and lucrative idea—until 2020.

THE POWER OF THE PAUSE

It was like a record scratching and the music coming to an abrupt stop. COVID hit. My business—built around gyms and water sports—got wiped. Six figures to zero, just like that. I had money in the bank but no clarity and no idea when things *might* go back to normal.

So I sat in front of my computer one morning in June and asked myself, "Is it time to quit?"

I decided I'd at least see what my options were. I applied for a job as a business analyst. No MBA. No formal experience. Just hard-won wisdom and grit. I got hired and traveled the country, mid-pandemic, helping small businesses stay alive. I was very often the only one in the airplane terminal, but I loved what I was doing, and in my first year I was able to show my clients over three million dollars in growth collectively. But I also saw something else: *My health was deteriorating.* I was overweight, depressed, and disconnected, all because I'd stopped applying empathy to the one person who needed it most—*me*.

I went home to Orlando and thankfully found the Celebrity Branding Agency. And finally, the pieces clicked. My purpose was never about the product. It was about the *people*. Coaching, branding, marketing—it all came back to helping people climb their own mountains. I wasn't here to be the star. I was here to be the sherpa who could help others reach their summit.

Zig Ziglar said, "You can get everything in life you want if you will just help enough other people get what they want."[1] That became my mission. Empathy became my method. The train was finally staying on the tracks. And the best part? About five years ago I got a call. It was my daughter. She was in town and asked me to lunch. I hadn't seen her in years, so it was awkward at first. Then, mid-bite, she looked up and said, "I know my mom's a bitch and that you wanted to be there for me. I get it."

I couldn't help but smile and say, "I've been waiting for twenty years to hear you say that."

Of all the conversations I've had in my life, that one was the greatest—not because it erased the past but because it proved that when you *flip your script*, when you stop performing and start connecting, when you choose empathy over ego, redemption becomes a very real thing. That's how you stop being the passive antagonist in your own script and write yourself a plot you can be proud of.

ENDNOTE

1.   "Zig Ziglar Quotes," Goodreads, accessed May 1, 2025, https://www.goodreads.com/author/quotes/50316.Zig_Ziglar?page=4.

About JT

Born at a young age with an innate passion for health and fitness, JT embarked on a journey that has spanned over fifteen years, transforming lives and businesses along the way. It all began in the high-energy world of personal training, where JT honed his skills working with MMA fighters and young athletes. This early experience ignited a profound commitment to fostering peak performance, setting the stage for a diverse and impactful career.

Driven by an entrepreneurial spirit, JT ventured into uncharted waters—literally—as he became the fifth-ever World Stand Up Paddleboard Association certified paddleboarding instructor on the East Coast. This milestone marked the beginning of a series of innovative business endeavors. His journey continued with Knockerball USA and Action Archery—Combat Archery, where JT not only embraced but thrived in the challenge of pioneering new and exciting recreational sports.

Throughout these ventures JT's core mission remained unchanged: to empower individuals to achieve their highest potential. This unwavering dedication eventually led him back to his true calling—coaching. Now, as a business and branding consultant, JT seamlessly blends his rich background in health and fitness with his entrepreneurial expertise to guide clients toward personal and professional success.

JT's coaching philosophy is rooted in the belief that true success stems from a harmonious balance between business strategies and personal health. He has helped countless clients not only climb the ladders of their careers but also enrich their lives with vitality and confidence. His unique approach has been transformative, leaving an indelible impact on those he works with.

Accolades and certifications underscore JT's expertise and commitment to personal development. His journey is peppered with personal anecdotes that speak to his resilience and innovation, from training athletes to navigating the fast-paced world of business innovation. Each step has reinforced his dedication to helping others achieve their goals.

As JT continues to inspire and lead, his story is a testament to the power of passion and perseverance. Whether he's helping a start-up define its brand or guiding a professional to better health and productivity, JT remains a beacon for those seeking to elevate every aspect of their lives. His journey isn't just about the milestones; it's about the people he's empowered along the way.

If you'd like to get in touch with JT, you can reach him at 423-301-0910, www.jthasyourback.com, or www.facebook.com/coachjthasyourback.

CHAPTER 17

THE ORANGE SWAN

By Jeffrey Andrew Luhrsen

My stomach lurched as soon as I saw the envelope. It was from a law firm known for its aggressive tactics. Inside was a letter that would temporarily blow up my life.

Years earlier I'd entered into what I thought was a strategic partnership with another attorney. He had dominated the local market for years, and when I moved to Florida in the late '90s to build my practice, I saw an opportunity for mutual benefit. In time I purchased his firm. But years later he changed his mind— and wanted a piece of it back. The problem wasn't the business logistics. It was our values. Mine had evolved, his hadn't, and I had no interest in continuing our partnership. As majority shareholder, I wanted him out. I didn't realize it then, but what I was dealing with wasn't just a financial disagreement; it was a collision of *Orange Swans*.

In negotiation the Black Swan is a hidden fact that changes everything. But there's another bird that no one talks about—the *Orange Swan*. You see, colors are symbolic. Orange is often associated with warmth, approachability, friendliness, in other words— connection. If orange is the color of connection, then the *Orange Swan* is the emotional thread that links us. It's the unspoken need that, once seen, dissolves walls. When you spot someone's *Orange Swan*, you're not just understanding them—you're meeting them. Not at the level of words, but at the level of *identity*.

The *Orange Swan* is the story we tell ourselves about what we need in order to feel safe, seen, or successful. It's invisible. Personal. Psychological. But it drives every decision we make.

Clinical and cognitive psychologists have studied stealth motivational factors and identified five that often exist but are seldom apparent: significance, belonging, certainty, growth, and contribution. My business partner's *Orange Swan*? Significance.

He didn't just want money. He needed to matter. And when I said I no longer wanted to work with him, he didn't just hear rejection—he heard erasure. That envelope was his response. A retaliation cloaked in legalese. It accused me of misconduct, of manipulating nonprofit relationships, of profiting unethically. The accusations were false, but they were loud. The letter threatened a class-action suit using every client I'd ever represented as ammunition. This wasn't about justice. This was a hit. A calculated strike from someone who couldn't tolerate the story he was now telling himself—that he'd been dismissed, disrespected, diminished. That's the thing about *Orange Swans*: if you don't recognize them in others, you'll misread the conflict entirely.

The emotional and financial toll was staggering. At one point my legal fees had crept well beyond $750,000. My marriage was strained. My sense of self cracked open. I had spent a lifetime in courtrooms, but this was a different kind of trial. One I didn't feel prepared for.

So I turned inward—not to better understand others but to reclaim dominion over my own mind.

I started studying psychology, behavioral economics, neuroscience, and philosophy. I needed to understand why I had been so blind to someone else's internal war—and more urgently, how to stop waging one in my own head. I wasn't studying for insight. I was studying for survival. The case dragged on. Lies were repeated until they started sounding like truth. False evidence was paraded around as if it held weight. And while it all eventually collapsed under the weight of its own fabrication, the lesson it left behind was permanent. After eight grueling years the judge threw it out. The claims were found to be baseless and malicious. They were ordered to pay half a million in legal fees, but by then, I had paid something even more precious: my peace. And I was determined to get it back. Sure, they got me suspended for thirty days over a hyper-technical advertising thing and for offering financial help to a client who was about to lose everything. Lawyers are not allowed to give their clients any money, and I did it anyway. That was the line I crossed. I had a choice between their man-made rule and God's compassion commands. Oddly enough, I've come to be grateful that they punished me for my choice. It is rare enough, I think, that any of us has the opportunity to stand up for our beliefs in such a public forum.

That experience trained me to look beyond the surface of conflict and into the psyche beneath it. To listen for the unspoken narrative. To spot the *Orange Swan*. And most importantly, to confront my own.

JUST LISTEN

Some lawyers might bristle when they read this, but it's the truth: The courtroom is theater.

It's a strategic, high-stakes performance. Most attorneys walk into a courtroom thinking they're selling something. They're selling an idea, an argument, a carefully concocted version of the truth. But what they're really doing is selling *belief.* They're pitching a narrative, and reverse-engineering the facts to fit it. The story comes first; the evidence comes second. That's how I was trained too, until I met Alejandro. He was unlike anyone else in the trial world. Alejandro didn't teach me how to *sell* a story. He taught me how to *find* it. He said something that changed the way I approached everything—not just in court, but in life. He said, "There's a story that wants to tell itself. Your job is to get out of its way."

At first, I didn't get it. I was used to walking into a courtroom armed with bullet points and exhibits. But Alejandro showed me another way: Listen more than you speak. Observe more than you argue. Watch the witness. Watch the judge. Read the room person by person.

And that's when it clicked. The *Orange Swan* wasn't just about the surface-level facts. It was about the invisible beliefs, identities, and internal codes that people carry silently. Chris Voss' *tactical empathy* isn't just about understanding someone's argument—it's about understanding the narrative that lives inside their head, the one they won't say out loud but act out in *every* decision. You can't influence someone unless you first understand what they're protecting. And everyone is protecting their *Orange Swan*. What's the story *they* are carrying? What's the outcome that would make *them* feel seen and vindicated? What emotion is at work behind their arguments? What part of their mind am I hearing from? Amygdala? Pre-frontal cortex? A little neuroscience can go a very long way. That was the shift. I learned to go from pushing a story to *uncovering* it, because here's the truth: People don't respond to facts. They respond to *meaning*. And meaning comes from story.

Cognitive scientists back this up. According to Mark Turner, one of the foremost voices in cognitive psychology, story isn't just how we *entertain* ourselves. It's how we *understand* ourselves. In *The Literary Mind*, Turner wrote that the human mind is structured by narrative—that we don't think in abstract principles or data. We think in stories. We are hardwired for them.

Stories organize our experience. They help us make sense of what happens to us and what's going on around us. And in a courtroom—a place built on conflict and confusion—story isn't just useful, it's essential. It's how we can flip the script and take a jury from confusion to clarity and from reasonable doubt to final decision.

Once I internalized that, I changed everything. I stopped trying to convince people to believe what *I* believed. I started listening to what *they* needed to believe, and why. I stopped walking in with my own script and started walking in with curiosity. What's this judge tired of hearing? What's this witness longing to confess? What would make this juror feel like they did something good today? And then, I told *that* story.

Looking back, even in my own life, I had been trying to make the facts fit the narrative I wanted to believe. I wanted to believe that I was in control, that justice would always prevail, and that if I followed the rules, I'd always win. But the truth—the story that wanted to tell itself—was harder to swallow. I am not in control. Justice is flawed. The system can be hijacked. But the narrative that saved me wasn't the one I forced. It was the one I *found*. And finding that story, the real one, gave me back a power that couldn't be taken away even by the most ruthless opponent. And it made me a more empathetic and effective person. It sounds counterintuitive, but the most persuasive thing in the world isn't certainty. It's empathy. And in a world where everyone's trying to be heard, sometimes the most radical thing you can do is shut up and *listen*.

THE POWER OF SUBTEXT

Humans think in stories. Psychology, neuroscience, literature—all those disciplines land on the same truth: Narrative isn't just how we *express* ourselves, it's how we *understand* our world. But here's the catch: not every story we tell ourselves is useful. Sometimes we're responding to life through outdated scripts that sabotage our results. We invent subplots, enemies, and motives. We cast ourselves as the hero or victim without even realizing it. Our beliefs around these misguided stories inform everything we do and are responsible for most of our circumstances.

I saw this firsthand during what should've been a straightforward business deal. Three people, co-owners of multiple companies, were trying to part ways. They were burned out, financially strained and one of their real estate projects was already in foreclosure. It was clear that this partnership needed to end before they were all financially ruined, and my role was to convince one of them to walk away from his shares worth hundreds of thousands of dollars, for nothing in return. Tall order. On paper it was a non-starter. No amount of logic, data, or persuasion was going to get him there. But then he said something, almost in passing: "Through all of these trials and tribulations, I have never abandoned Pat."

That word—*abandoned*—lit something up in me. He had told me before that one of their companies was "veteran-owned and female-operated." I remembered thinking: that's not a marketing line, that's an *identity*. He was a veteran. My father, my brother, and I are all Marines. The code runs deep, and I know how soldiers talk. More importantly, I know how soldiers *think*.

And regular people don't talk about abandonment like that. Civilians don't carry that kind of weight around their choices. But soldiers? They don't abandon a mission when it gets hard, and they never leave people behind. Ever.

So I started digging—not with questions but with empathy. I didn't try to argue him out of or into any decision. I didn't try to sell him. I just mirrored back what I heard in the subtext of his story. "You know," I said, "that's not something a regular businessman says. That's something soldiers say." That was it. I never said another word about it. That single moment of validation—of being seen within the story that mattered to *him*—shifted everything. Not because I changed his mind, but because I acknowledged his *identity*. I found the *Orange Swan* and met him at the level of meaning, rather than logic.

People make decisions emotionally first. Then they rationalize them afterward. That's why the real conversation is always happening *beneath* the words. The real negotiation is about what someone needs to believe to feel like the hero of their own story. Or at the very least—not the villain. In his mind, walking away from the deal felt like abandoning the mission, which didn't sit right with his personal code or ethics. But after I saw the *Orange Swan* in him, he reframed the whole question and decided that he would let go. He never gave his reasons, and I never asked. It was his call and was always going to be his call. In tuning into his personal code, I met him at the level of *identity*. And that's where the *Orange Swan* lives.

SEEK FIRST TO UNDERSTAND

It sounds simple. But in a world flooded with noise, ego, and projection, it might be the hardest—and most vital—thing we ever learn to do. Clarity and humility are priceless, but you can't swipe a credit card for them. Not even for seven hundred billion dollars—the amount America pours into higher education every year. And still, we fail to understand one another. Talk past each other. And to my knowledge it's not possible to major in empathy and minor in self-awareness.

We praise emotional intelligence, write entire chapters on active listening, build corporate workshops around communication, and yet 91 percent of us think we're great listeners, while 70 percent say the people closest to us are terrible at it. That disconnect is not a skill gap. It's a *perception* gap. It's a fear-driven refusal to stop telling and selling long enough to *listen*.

The courtroom taught me that. In a high-stakes case there are accusations, betrayals, and mischaracterizations. But I've learned that I'm most successful when I don't try to be the loudest voice in the room and instead have the most empathetic presence. Because there are *Orange Swans*—hidden truths—in everyone's self-narrative. There are wounds and codes and values they never talk about but might - if given the space. I have found, anecdotally, that people *want* to reveal their *Orange Swan*-what makes them different. Epley (2021) published *Miscalibrated Expectations Create a Barrier to Deeper Conversation*, a study that discovered that people enjoy deep conversations with strangers! Shipley's work also shows that we overestimate awkwardness and underestimate the joy of deep conversations with strangers, so relax. Give someone a chance to tell their truth and they just may do it.

Here's the lesson I experienced, and the one I offer to you: People don't operate based on information. They operate based on narrative. You can't out-argue someone's identity. You can't outmaneuver their core need to be the hero of their own story. But if you can see the *Orange Swan*—the story they're trying to protect—you can connect in a way that transcends strategy. You can listen in a way that disarms. You can lead in a way that heals.

Ask yourself, "What story is this person inhabiting?"

Once you take the time to understand their story, you earn the right to help them write a new one. And *that* is how you flip the script. You stop trying to force an agenda and let the story that *wants* to be told come through. In the end we can "fight" for justice, or we can strive to create the conditions in which it naturally materializes. Often the truth that changes everything isn't the one we argue for. It's the *Orange Swan* we're finally willing to hear.

About Jeffrey

There are some things that Jeffrey Andrew Luhrsen has done, but achievements alone do not always reveal who a person really is or what they are like. Jeffrey has been a Marine Corps NCO, a scholarship winner in undergraduate school, an Army officer and paratrooper, a scholarship winner and honors graduate from law school, a law clerk for a federal judge, a judge advocate of the US Army, a special assistant US attorney, lead trial counsel in hundreds of civil cases, a widely published legal writer, a business executive, a member of The National Academy of Bestselling Authors, and what Temple University calls a Master of Trial Advocacy. Trial judges and opposing lawyers give his legal ability and ethical standards the highest possible rating, "AV Preeminent®" on the Martindale-Hubbell scale. With over thirty years of live courtroom experience, Jeffrey Luhrsen is an attorney who understands the power of timing and presentation.

Jeffrey's temperament, called Architect, is the rarest of the sixteen recognized by Kiersey or Myers-Briggs, embracing only 1–2 percent of the population. Jeffrey's particular gift is Architectonics, the "systematization of knowledge"— organizing, structuring, building, and configuring work flows, methods, models, and systems that work. In a profession where flamboyance is generally preferred over research, Jeffrey is happy to retreat into a world of books and emerge only when physical needs become imperative!

Following his post–Juris Doctor studies, he became interested in the science behind human decision-making, which led him first to behavioral economics and eventually to cognitive psychology, neuroscience, neuroeconomics, and the science of storytelling. Like others with his rare temperament, he is insatiably curious. Among other things, he discovered that people respond to *meaning*, not facts, and meaning comes from story. Stories are not just how we *entertain* ourselves, but rather how we *understand* ourselves and organize our experiences.

Chris Voss' paradigm-shifting book, *Never Split the Difference*, has exerted enormous influence over Jeffrey's approach to business and life. Always building on truths already known, Jeffrey thinks that Voss' Black Swan Method™ systematizes listening and emotional intelligence.

However, Jeffrey knows that the voices people hear when they are considering their options are actually *stories*, and the stories people tell themselves drive *all* their decisions. Jeffrey's gift is hearing unspoken stories and working within those frames.

There are many lawyers but only one like him.

CHAPTER 18

TENSION IS LEVERAGE

By Trenton Wisecup

Nineteen years. That's how long my mother has been in bed. She wasn't always like this. After my younger sister was born, she developed a rare back disease that quickly stole her mobility and her independence. My dad became the sole provider, working constantly just to keep us afloat. That meant that there was no one in the stands at my football games, no family at my graduation, and on Senior Night, I walked onto the field by myself.

I was sad, and yet I never felt totally alone.

You see my mom was my biggest inspiration, and I could feel her presence in those moments. It broke her heart, but *her* extraordinary strength to carry on helped *me* stay strong without her. She taught me a lot of what I know about hard work. Before her back went out, she homeschooled me. When I had to go to public school, I was in second grade, reading and writing at a fifth-grade level.

I decided early on that I wasn't going to feel sorry for myself. I was going to make my parents proud. I was determined to achieve success so my mom could live through me.

That mindset got me through a lot. Some people learn mental toughness through books and mentors. I learned it through necessity. I couldn't afford to fall apart. Resilience and determination weren't things I chose to learn—they were things I had to *live*. But it wasn't always smooth sailing.

My dad was my first leadership coach, and he tried to drill this into me. When I was young, I partied a lot and made some bad decisions. My dad would say to me, "I'm raising you to be a leader. What are you doing?" At the time, I shrugged it off. Then, at twenty-one, something finally clicked. I called him and said, "Were you right about *everything*?"

I decided to buckle down and build the kind of success I could be proud of. In 2017 I founded Arrow Roofing Services. Since then, we've served over two thousand Michigan residents, delivering on our word, our work, and our reputation. Some lessons in leadership came naturally; others had to be sharpened by mentors like Sam Taggart—a guy who didn't just teach sales, but how to build something bigger than yourself; scaling a team, crafting a vision, drilling down on core values. But the drive? That was always in me. And I would need every bit to close the deals, grow the business and navigate one of the toughest conversations of my life!

KEEPING FOCUS WHEN EMOTIONS ARE HIGH

The hardest negotiations aren't the ones with strangers. They're the ones where emotions are already in the room and the other side is someone you know. A spouse. A family member. A best friend. That's where most people lose. They lose focus and let emotions take over.

I learned this the hard way.

At twenty-one I owned my own business. I couldn't afford to hire experienced professionals, so I hired my friends. And that's where the first test came: how do you balance friendship and leadership? When are we friends, and when are we at work? For me, it was simple—at work, we're at work. That clarity, however, wasn't shared. There was slacking. The guys weren't knocking on enough doors, taking action, or showing up the way they needed to. And because we were friends, it was assumed I'd look the other way. For two years I let it slide. But then came the breaking point— Summer 2020. COVID shut our state down, and I had to make a move. I relocated my operation to Akron, Ohio, where business was still open. I rented a house and for nine months, we lived together, worked together, woke up together. It was total immersion. And that's when everything boiled over.

My massive level of action exposed their lack of it. The gap became obvious, and with it came jealousy, animosity, and resentment. Suddenly I couldn't give criticism or offer mentorship. Any feedback was taken as an attack. My employees, who were my friends, started having bad attitudes, trying to manipulate me and displaying dominance tactics that built tension thick enough to cut with a knife.

One of these guys was my best friend. I avoided confrontation because I was afraid of losing the friendship, but it hit me—was he even my friend at this point? Were any of them?

I was so focused on not hurting anyone else that I was betraying myself. That's a rookie mistake and at some point, avoiding conflict isn't just avoidance—it's weakness. If I didn't *take* control, they would *keep* it!

I prepared. I got my mindset where it needed to be and wrote down the most important things I wanted to talk about. I was determined to keep my cool. My dad always taught me that between glad and sad is the neutral zone—that's where business happens. If you get emotional, you lose. When emotions are high, logic is low. You pay a penalty for reacting emotionally.

This wasn't about friends anymore. It was about metrics, facts and performance. If I let them twist the narrative or veer off into personal territory, I'd lose sight of the real objective.

And that's the lesson. In negotiations—whether it's with a business partner, a spouse, or your own kids—you stick to the goal. You stay on topic. You don't get distracted by anything else.

The second you do? You've already lost.

SEE BEYOND THE SURFACE

Negotiation is an awkward sport. When you step into a tough conversation, you can confidently expect silence, discomfort, and resistance. When I had to confront my best friend, it wasn't just about business. It was about breaking through layers of denial, entitlement, and old patterns of thinking. And that's where most people screw up—they go in frustrated, angry, ready to fight. But that's not how you win. I had to step back and ask myself, "Why is he acting this way?" He had never had a real job outside of working for me. He had never been held accountable in a professional setting. He was an only child, born into a wealthy family, used to a world where effort didn't always equal results. Not because he was a bad person—but because that was all he had ever known. And once I realized that I couldn't be angry. I couldn't judge him. If I had grown up the same way, I might behave the same way too.

Instead of making it personal, I made it clear. I put myself in his shoes and saw the situation for what it really was. He wasn't slacking because he didn't care. He was slacking because he had never been in an environment where effort mattered. He didn't even realize what he was doing. At first, he flat-out denied it, which is human nature. But I didn't react. I held the line. I said to him, "If the roles were reversed, and you owned this business, you would never catch me slacking. I would work twice as hard for you, because we're friends." That hit him.

It wasn't immediate, but over time something shifted. When we came back from Akron, I distanced myself from the ones who didn't want to grow. They made him pick a side. And he did.

Today, he's still with me—not just as my best friend, but as the lead roofing systems expert of a seven-figure company we built from the ground up. That's the power of real empathy. It's not about letting things slide or being nice. It's about seeing the truth beneath the excuses and staying calm in the face of confrontation—because for true leaders, the hardest conversations aren't about calling people out. They're about calling them up.

THE ART OF NOT TAKING THE BAIT

In 2021 I knocked on the door of a homeowner whose house had been wrecked by a massive hailstorm. From the moment he opened the door, I could tell this was going to be a battle. He was hard-nosed and not happy. What I've learned though is that the hardest ones to win pay you the fastest. The toughest customers always start with resistance. They've been burned before, so they put up walls. But if you stay patient, and don't let your ego take over, those same people turn into your best clients.

I started my pitch, and within minutes, he started countering. A contractor had screwed him over with missed deadlines, broken promises, and a mess that left a bad taste in his mouth.

At that moment, I had two choices: push back and fight his resistance or sidestep it completely.

So I said, "Listen, I'm going to pick on you for two seconds if you'll let me. Imagine I'm the new hot girl at school, and you just got out of a bad relationship. You've got trust issues, and I get it. But now that you and I are starting a new relationship, is it fair to project that last experience onto me? I haven't broken your trust."

He laughed! That was the moment I broke through. I had empathy without pressure. I validated his frustration, but never let myself get emotional back. I knew what he was doing—he wanted me to fight. He wanted to poke me with a stick, rattle me, and get me upset. But I wasn't there to fight—I was there to *help*. Most people lose deals like this because they take it personally. They get defensive, puff up their ego, and let their emotions override their goal. They don't recognize that the anger isn't even directed at them. The customer is mad at the last guy, mad at the situation, and mad at the hassle, not at you.

I let him vent, beat his chest and air out every frustration, because once all that energy was spent, I had everything I needed—the leverage, the information, the real pain point: trust.

And that's where patience wins. At that point, I looked him in the eye and said, "If I didn't think you were perfect for this, I would've walked away thirty minutes ago. But I see how much you value your property. You're the exact kind of person I want to work for, and I want to earn your business." That was it. He wanted the roof done in forty days. I told him I'd do it in thirty after approval. We delivered, he paid, and he became one of my best referral sources.

Most people would have walked away the moment he got aggressive. They would have let their ego flare up, told themselves they didn't deserve to be yelled at, and lost the sale. I knew better. If you let yourself get triggered, you lose. If you stay patient and remember you are there to help not win, the win happens by default.

The Million-Dollar Door

If you've ever been hunting, you know it can be both one of the most relaxing sports of all time and the most frustrating! Hunting has taught me more about business than any book ever could. It's the ultimate test of patience, discipline, and knowing when to seize an opportunity. There's an old saying in hunting: "Don't pass up on the first day what you'd take on the last."

In other words—don't wait for the perfect moment, because it may never come.

Too many business owners are in a constant rush. They want results now. They chase, they push, they grind, but in nature, that's not how it works. You're not in control. You have to wait, watch, and allow the mission to unfold. Sometimes, you sit for hours and see nothing. Does that mean you never go again? Of course not. Because the next time, the opportunity might be right in front of you. That's exactly how sales work.

I once knocked on the door of a massive house, pitched the guy for 15 minutes, and closed the deal without a single negotiation. Just like that, sale done. But what happened next was the real lesson. Right after he agreed, he asked, "Have you heard of Bitcoin?" At the time, I scoffed and said, "Yeah, it's a total scam!" He smiled and said, "I'm going to change your life today." Most people would have left immediately after closing the sale. I stayed and listened.

That conversation led to him mentoring me in crypto and

because I took the time to be patient and stay open, that one knock turned into something bigger. I'm now a crypto millionaire. I call these Million-Dollar Doors. You never know what's on the other side. It could be a sale, a partnership, or a life-changing lesson. But if you're only focused on winning and leaving, you'll miss it.

Flipping the script isn't just about getting people to see your point of view. It's about being willing to have the script flipped on *you*! Opportunity is all around you. The question is, Will you recognize it when it appears, or will you, having gotten what you came for, prematurely walked out of a million-dollar door?

THE LAW OF ACTION—OPPORTUNITY BELONGS TO THE BOLD

The world loves to talk about *manifestation* and visualizing success, but let's be real—the universe isn't your magic genie. There's truth in the law of attraction, but too many people take it as an excuse to sit back and wait. They think about success, they dream about it, but they never take action. And that's the problem. Because manifestation without execution is just daydreaming.

The law of action is different. It's not about wishing—it's about *moving*. It's about recognizing that opportunity responds to motion. It's about knocking on that extra door, staying in the conversation an extra five minutes, and refusing to let hesitation kill momentum. But action alone isn't enough. Especially in negotiations. Mental toughness is what keeps you moving when things go south. Patience is what stops you from missing out on great deals. Empathy is what earns you long-term trust, not just short-term compliance.

That's how I built my business. That's how I turned one door knock into a multi-million-dollar opportunity. That's how I took tough conversations and turned them into defining moments in leadership and friendship. And that's why today, we're taking everything we've learned and packaging it into a system other business owners can use.

The SOLVEX Method isn't just a sales process—it's a modern approach to creating trust, designing a buying experience, and executing at the highest level. Whether it's our unique product, the GAF Timberline Solar Shingle, or any other high-ticket offer, the principles remain the same: Mental toughness. Patience. Strategic empathy. Clear execution.

At the end of the day success is waiting for *us* to move first—and to move with the drive, strength, and precision of a leader.

About Trenton

Industry Titan | Roofing and Solar Expert | Relentless Closer

Some people wait for success. Trenton hunts it down. Born into Section 8 housing, where rent was just twenty dollars a month, he didn't grow up with advantages—he built them. No college degree. No handouts. Just a relentless mindset, an obsession with winning, and the courage to take risks when others hesitated. At nineteen years old he stepped into door-to-door sales for one of the largest storm roofing companies in the US and didn't just hold his own—he took over. In his first year he became the number one sales producer, earning six figures, and proving that raw determination beats experience every single time. At twenty-one he bet on himself—hard. Instead of playing it safe, he launched his own roofing company, and within a year it was doing seven figures. By twenty-two he was a self-made millionaire.

Since then, he's personally generated over eight figures in lifetime sales, scaled and led teams of fifty-plus reps, and helped countless others experience massive spikes in closing rates, revenue, and mindset breakthroughs. In 2022 he was officially ranked the number one Roofing Door Knocker in the nation, winning the National Knocking League with his team, dominating an industry where only the strong survive. He's mastered high-ticket closing in any environment—on the doorstep, in the boardroom, or virtually. His personal best? Over seven figures in a single month. But Trenton doesn't just build businesses—he builds people, whether it's creating new systems, recruiting, training, or implementing technology to help dominate. Trenton is passionate about helping people succeed while becoming the best versions of themselves.

A true roofing and solar expert, he thrives on developing leaders, creating high-performance teams, and helping individuals shatter their personal and financial ceilings. His company is now ranked in the top 1 percent of all roofing businesses in the US, but he's not even close to finished. At twenty-eight, based in Michigan, he continues to dominate, scale, and set the standard in sales and business leadership. While others fear risk, he runs toward it. While most make excuses, he makes impact. While many hesitate, he takes massive action.

If you're looking to master the art of closing, scaling your business, or developing a mindset that makes you unstoppable, Trenton is the one you want in your corner, because in his world there's no ceiling—only the next level.

CHAPTER 19

BLACK BELT NEGOTIATION

Winning Without Throwing the First Punch

By Scott L. Frost

It's hard to believe that one phone call could change the trajectory of three lives. I was in law school chasing the dream I'd built for myself with the support of my parents. Then one day my mom called, and I could tell by her voice that something was very wrong. She was too calm, the kind of calm that tells you bad news is coming. "It's your dad," she said. "They let him go. We aren't going to be able to support you in school anymore."

I was completely shocked. Fired! Not for incompetence or lack of results. Quite the opposite. He was *too* good. Too experienced. Too expensive. Thirty years of climbing the ladder, from back-breaking labor to the executive suite—gone in an instant. And I couldn't do a damn thing about it. Growing up, we weren't rich, but we always had more than enough. My dad had worked two jobs for as long as I could remember—days in sales, nights and weekends running cattle and horses on our small Kentucky farm. He'd built something great for us, and there was always a sense of security. Until suddenly there wasn't. My father, the man who taught me how to shake a hand, build relationships, and read people before they even spoke, was suddenly unemployed and so ashamed of it he didn't even tell me himself.

He wasn't the same after that. The easy confidence, the warmth that made everyone gravitate toward him—it all faded. For six months he was a shadow of himself, as though a light had been snuffed out. The change in *him* lit a fire in *me*. I'd always thought

I'd go into criminal law, but watching my father, a man who had built his life brick by brick, have it all ripped away by a faceless corporation—that was personal.

This wasn't just about one job loss. It was about identity, dignity, and what happens when the powerful decide you're disposable. This was what happened when corporations decided that numbers on a spreadsheet meant more than years of dedication and expertise. Now, I wasn't just going to practice law. I was going to arm myself with the skills to fight for people like my father—people who built something, only to have it stolen. And if I was going to take on corporate giants, I'd need to learn how to negotiate as though life was at stake. Because for the people I'd be fighting for, it was.

A New Weapon

The military had always fascinated me. As a kid, I devoured books on warfare and strategy, obsessed with George S. Patton, studying *The Art of War* and applying those lessons to everything I did— including earning my black belt in karate. I had my sights set on West Point but didn't realize you needed a congressional nomination to get in. Coming from a small town in Kentucky, a place with one stop sign, my family wasn't politically connected. When I went for my physical at Xavier University, the officers there told me straight: My chances without that nomination were slim. But they also gave me another option—ROTC. Xavier offered me a scholarship, and in return, I owed the Army three years of active duty. I gave them six.

I was a federal prosecutor in the Army, handling everything from fraud to capital murder cases. One case changed how I saw everything.

It was a double homicide involving gang members, and one agent stood out. He had a *knack* for getting people to confess. Time and time again, he cracked cases by getting people to say things against their own interests. It was like magic. I had to know how he did it, so I asked.

His answer? *Mirroring, patience,* and *empathy.* He listened. He labeled their emotions. He gave them space, acknowledged what they felt, and in doing so made them feel *heard.* The more they talked, the more they trusted. And when they trusted, they confessed. It was the opposite of what I had been taught to believe. It wasn't about force. It wasn't about intimidation. The best interrogators and negotiators weren't the ones who barked orders. They were the ones who created an environment where people *wanted* to talk.

I saw it in the military too when dealing with suspects. The movies had it all wrong—threats, aggression, brute force? None of it worked. The ones who got results were the ones who used patience, rapport, and respect. That fascinated me. Everything I thought I knew about power, persuasion, and winning shifted. And now, in learning this skill, I had a new weapon. And I was going to need it because I was going home to fight the giants.

MASTERING THE ART OF NO-DEMAND NEGOTIATIONS

A black belt in karate doesn't win by overpowering an opponent with brute force. They win with patience, precision, and the ability to read every subtle shift in their adversary's stance. They wait, they adapt, and when the moment is right, they strike with calculated efficiency.

Strategic negotiation is no different. Today, I am the owner of Frost Law Firm, helping families that have been victimized by corporations, and my training as a black belt has come in handy.

You see, the most effective negotiators don't rush or demand or reveal their hand too soon. They control the tempo. They use tactical empathy to understand the other side's fears, pressures, and motivations. And when the other side is expecting a fight, they step back and let them punch air.

That's how I won one of my biggest cases.

My client had dedicated his entire life to a company, and what did he get in return? Mesothelioma—the asbestos cancer. The company hadn't taken safety precautions, and they knew it. They also knew that if this case went to a jury, they'd be on the hook for a massive verdict. They wanted to settle. *Fast.* They expected the usual back-and-forth—an opening demand, a counteroffer, a tug-of-war over numbers. That's how the game is usually played, but I had no intention of playing by their rules. So when their attorney asked for a number, I simply said, "The family wants a lot."

"A lot? How much is a lot?" they asked. "A lot," I said. I refused to name a number. Every time they asked, I just said, "More." I listened. I empathized. I acknowledged that their position was tough because their client was fully exposed, but I never gave them a number to push against, and that made them anxious. They weren't used to that. They were used to negotiating within a framework, knowing their target, anchoring a figure, working the margins. Without a number, they were negotiating with a ghost. Eventually they started bidding against themselves. Offer after offer, they kept raising the number, waiting for me to finally engage. I didn't. I just kept saying, "More." After a month of this they called and said, "We went to the CEO for authorization. This has *got* to be enough money." I could hear the desperation in their voices. They had exhausted every option and gone higher than they ever had before. In that moment, I knew we had taken every last dollar off the table.

This is the power of patience and tactical empathy. Negotiation isn't about demanding. It's about guiding. It's about creating an environment where the other side feels pressure to move, even when you haven't made a single demand. Just as in martial arts, the best move is often no move at all—until the perfect moment. And by then, the fight is already won.

KEEP YOUR "ENEMIES" CLOSER

One of the highest-stakes conversations I have as a trial lawyer happens before the trial even begins—when I pick a jury. It is unpredictable, is filled with risk, and requires a level of strategic empathy that can make or break a case. Every jury is different.

Most jurors don't want to be there. They see it as an inconvenience, something forced upon them. Others *do* want to be there but for the wrong reasons, hoping to push their own version of justice, often in ways that help no one. Walking into jury selection is like walking onto a battlefield where you don't control the terrain. The wrong move or assumption, and the case can be lost before a single argument is made. That's why it's not about control but understanding.

One of my toughest jury selections involved a retrial after an appeal. In the jury pool sat an insurance adjuster, exactly the kind of juror most lawyers representing injured families want to strike immediately. These are people who evaluate claims for a living and are conditioned to think in terms of minimizing payouts, not maximizing justice. But when I read their jury questionnaire, something caught my attention. Their answers weren't as rigid as I expected. There was something there, maybe a crack in the usual armor. I had a choice. I could take the safe route, dismiss them, and move on. Or I could take the risk. Most lawyers would go on the attack in questioning—challenge the adjuster, force them to admit bias, push them into a corner.

But I didn't. Instead, I got curious. "What makes you good at your job?" I asked. They spoke about their ability to assess situations quickly, analyze risk, and see through people who were just out for money. That was my opening. "That's got to be exhausting," I said, "dealing with people every day who just want something from you." I saw their posture shift. I had said out loud what they probably felt but rarely heard acknowledged. And then they told me the truth: They *hated* their job. I didn't argue. I didn't push. I just listened. I let them feel heard. And when I finally asked if they could give my client a fair trial, I believed their answer. I took the risk and left them on the jury.

It would have been easy to play it safe and strike that juror, but empathy—real, strategic empathy—means seeing people beyond their roles and labels and recognizing the deeper motivations at play. Risk is uncomfortable. But the biggest wins come from understanding the person on the other side, not confronting them. That's true in trial law. It's true in negotiation. It's true in life. But I'd be lying if I said I wasn't nervous.

THE LESSON IN ASSUMPTIONS

Throughout the eight-week trial I was convinced I had made a mistake.

The insurance adjuster—the juror I had taken a risk on—sat in the front row with their arms crossed the entire time. No visible reaction, no signs of sympathy, nothing. Just stone-faced silence. Every day, I watched them, second-guessing my decision. Had I misread them? Had I blown my chance at justice for my client? But I had made my choice, and now I had to work with it. Rather than write them off, I leaned in to what I *did* know. I thought about their experience—What in their world might resonate with my client's struggle? What common ground could we find?

We crafted testimony that spoke to their reality. We asked witnesses to make subtle, nonverbal connections—eye contact at key moments, slight gestures that signaled respect and understanding. We paid attention to every flicker of body language. And yet the juror remained stoic. When the jury returned with a verdict in our favor, I was relieved—but what happened next *shocked* me. The strongest advocate had been the one I doubted the most.

After the trial, the insurance adjuster sent us a note. They had known we were skeptical of them from the start. They had felt it but wanted us to know that despite our doubts they had been committed to doing the right thing—not just under the law but for the sake of *humanity*.

They had been our *strongest* juror. The very person I feared would work against us had been the one fighting the hardest for us in deliberations. It's easy to put people into boxes and assume that an insurance adjuster will always side with the defense. Other lawyers thought we were *crazy* for keeping people like that on our juries. But time and time again, we've learned that when you treat people like humans, acknowledge their struggles and frustrations, and listen instead of lecture—they surprise you. People want to be heard. They want their experiences to be understood. And when they feel that respect, they are more likely to return it. The biggest lesson in empathy isn't just about understanding others—it's about understanding *ourselves.*

When we assume the worst about someone, what does that say about *us?* What biases are we carrying? What stories have we told ourselves about who people are and what they believe?

The real power of tactical empathy is that it forces us to look inward. To challenge our own judgments, step outside of our own experiences and ask, "What led this person to where they are?" And the deeper we go, the better we become—not just as lawyers but as humans.

STANDING FOR WHAT'S RIGHT: THE FIGHT THAT NEVER ENDS

I didn't set out to be a fighter. But life has a way of choosing your battles for you.

I've spent my career standing up for people who had everything taken from them—by corporations, by systems built to protect the powerful, by a world that too often values profit over people. But long before I ever stepped into a courtroom, I learned the most important lesson of all: *No one wins alone.*

That lesson started with my father, a man who gave everything to his job, only to be discarded as if he didn't matter. He taught me that dignity isn't given—it's *earned.* And when someone tries to take it away, you either let them, or you stand up and fight. It continued in the military, where I saw what war does—not just to nations but to people. Where I learned that true power isn't in dominance but in *understanding.* Where I saw firsthand that even in the darkest places people look to those who will fight for them. And it carried through to every case I've ever tried, every negotiation I've ever walked into, every jury I've ever stood before.

I've learned that sometimes the best way to win is to *listen*. To step back when the other side expects you to attack and let them reveal their own weaknesses. To let them make the first move while you wait for the right moment. In the end the world doesn't change when people play it safe. It changes when someone understands that the real fight isn't about crushing the opposition; it's about seeing the battlefield through their eyes, mastering their fears, and using that insight to turn conflict into victory.

About Scott

Scott Frost is a US Army veteran, dedicated worker advocate, and experienced trial lawyer. He began his journey in Ames, Iowa, before moving frequently during his childhood, eventually settling in Kentucky. He earned an ROTC scholarship to Xavier University and later obtained his law degree from the University of Kentucky, where he was a member of the National Moot Court Team that won regional honors and competed nationally.

After law school Scott served as a Judge Advocate in the US Army, where he worked as a prosecutor, defense counsel, and Special Assistant US Attorney. His military legal career culminated in handling a federal capital murder trial. Upon leaving the Army, he shifted his focus to asbestos litigation, trying mesothelioma cases across the country. A graduate of the prestigious Trial Lawyers College, Scott remains deeply committed to advancing trial advocacy.

Beyond the courtroom Scott and his wife, Kimberly, are proud parents of three. He is dedicated to the pursuit of justice—both in his career and in the legacy he leaves for future generations.

CHAPTER 20

THE ANATOMY OF A STALEMATE

By Rebecca Tedder

The hotel room was dark and silent except for the hum of the air conditioner. My phone buzzed beside me, another calendar alert, another conference call. I blinked at the ceiling, trying to orient myself. Was I in LA? New York? Maybe Chicago. It didn't matter. The landscape had changed again, but the script hadn't. For years I'd been traveling nonstop, and that morning, I couldn't remember what day it was, where I'd just come from or what city I was in. It was time for a change.

Before that moment of reckoning, I had spent years navigating the power dynamics of media distribution—CNN, UCTV, MTV. I had interviewed celebrities, closed several deals worth multimillions, and walked nearly every red carpet you can name. I knew how to navigate the game and learned more every day. I was comfortable sitting across from a room full of suits and naming my number, straight-faced or with a smile, without flinching. I knew how to move the needle with a calm strength without ever raising my voice.

Eventually, I traded in that relentless pace for something that felt more like purpose. I launched a few of my own companies— International Associates, Fearless Capital, and Human Upgrade— to help others communicate with more precision, power, and clarity. But make no mistake, those years in the trenches tested me and shaped me into who I am today. They sharpened my instincts and taught me the single most valuable skill a woman in business can have—the skills of communication and the art of negotiation. Now, whether I'm guiding a client to greenlight a campaign, advising on a high-stakes merger, or convincing a friend to take the leap she's afraid to take, I know exactly what to say, how to say it, and the precise moment someone's mindset shifts. Negotiation isn't just a skill. It's a language. And I'd become fluent.

I became a negotiator by necessity, long before I made it my career. My childhood was a masterclass in adaptation. My father worked for IBM. Anyone who works for IBM knows it's an acronym for "I've been moved," so my childhood was a blur of new faces and new social ecosystems. Every new school was a fresh negotiation. That's where I first learned the value of observation and how much people reveal when they're resisting something unfamiliar. Later, I came to understand that resistance isn't the enemy of progress, it's a byproduct of it. Whether it's digital transformation, corporate culture shifts, or personal reinvention, people don't resist *change* itself. They resist what change represents: uncertainty and loss of control.

In every negotiation there's a moment where things stop moving. The energy shifts. Someone leans back or crosses their arms, or says, "I don't know," but what they really mean is "I'm not ready." That's resistance. And it's the most important part of the conversation.

Most people see resistance as a wall. I see it as a map, a subtle signal that tells me where the fear lives or what the other side feels is under threat. The moment someone begins to explain their resistance, I know we're getting close to a solution, not because they've agreed to anything yet but because they've stopped posturing and started revealing what's *real*.

This is what I do. I'm a facilitator and negotiator by trade, but my passion is understanding what's not being said—human behavior, cognitive bias, and the science of change. I hold a master's degree in industrial psychology, a string of advanced certifications in communication and applied behavioral theory, but long before I had the degrees or the titles, I was studying resistance. Chester

Karass once wrote, "In life, you don't get what you deserve. You get what you negotiate." He was right.

In my work, especially in mergers and acquisitions, or as a strategic fixer brought in when deals stall, I rely on frameworks like Chris Voss' tactical empathy and my own behavioral models to identify what's driving the tension in the room. People come guarded. They come with agendas. But beneath that is usually a simple truth: they are resisting something. And that tension? It isn't the problem. It's the doorway.

WHAT RESISTANCE REALLY STANDS FOR

Resistance doesn't always look like an argument. Sometimes it comes in the form of a closed mouth and a closed mind. Sometimes it shows up in the form of unchallenged traditions and stubborn beliefs. I see it every day in M&A. Every owner believes their company is worth millions more than the market shows, and every buyer wants a deal. Both sides walk in clutching their version of the truth. That's when I step in—not to break the stalemate but to build the bridge. After all, the etymology of the word *negotiate* finds its roots in the Latin negotiatus, which means "to carry on." That's the goal—to carry on, move forward, make *progress*.

And to do that, you have to learn. I don't walk into a room swinging. I walk in *curious*. I ask questions. I listen for what's not being said. What do they fear *losing*? What do they *need* to walk away with to feel like they won? What human drives, emotional currents, and underlying motivations are running the show?

Years ago I had just left CTN and had been recruited to a prominent media firm in New York. I wasn't new to pressure or performance, and now I was stepping into the role of overseeing *distribution*, the engine behind the scenes that moves stock prices and determines bonuses. At my first meeting, however, three senior men asked me to get their coffee. They saw me and slotted me right into a role I hadn't signed up for. It wasn't intentional, it was just natural resistance. They weren't used to seeing a woman my age running a multimillion-dollar division.

And that wasn't the last time resistance showed up.

At the time, I was traveling constantly. The weather was brutal and back then, there was no Uber. You had to stand outside like every other freezing New Yorker and hope to hail a cab. So, I found a better way. I booked a car service. It saved time, was actually less expensive than a cab, and it protected the firm's investment. I could show up on time for off-site meetings rather than showing up late, frazzled and soaked with rain. When the expense report came back flagged, my assistant told me there was "pushback on the limo service." Limo? It was a town car. But that wasn't the point. The point was: How dare I. Who did I think I was? It didn't matter that my solution saved them money. Logic doesn't always enter the room, at least not at first. Emotions, pride, and tradition tend to take the lead long before *reason* has a seat at the table. They weren't used to someone operating like I did. They were used to hierarchy. They *resisted* change even when it made total fiscal sense. I wasn't just negotiating a car service; I was negotiating the right to think differently and operate outside the expected structure. And I won.

That's the thing about resistance; it's not a signal to stop. It's a signal to *dig deeper*. To find the leverage. Whether it's a billion-dollar deal or a personal decision, resistance isn't something to bulldoze through. It's something to study. Respect. And when the time is right—*reframe*. Because once you understand what people are *really* protecting, you can finally show them what they have to gain.

WHY IS NEGOTIATION UNCOMFORTABLE

Most people find negotiation uncomfortable, not because they don't know what they want but because they don't know how to ask for it without creating conflict. The very word *negotiation* often conjures images of a battle of wills where someone wins and someone loses. That perception alone builds resistance. We instinctively resist conversations that feel like confrontations. Yet success in negotiating doesn't fall to the person who dominates the conversation, but to the one who *decodes* it.

At its core negotiation is an information game. The real power isn't in the volume of your voice but in the precision of your questions. The best negotiators I know aren't the ones who speak the most; they're the ones who *listen* the best—strategically, patiently, intentionally. They enter the conversation not with the goal of overpowering the other side, but with the goal of understanding them. They know resistance is just a signal that something *unspoken* is at stake.

The challenge is that most people walk into negotiations without a roadmap. They rely on gut instinct or outdated playbooks rooted in ego. Then, when the conversation veers off course—when emotion enters the room and logic goes out the window—they're left scrambling. Emotions often drive the decision-making process long before the numbers do. That's why having a structured approach is crucial. You can't wing your way through resistance.

Then there's the concept of fairness. In theory it sounds like a noble goal. In practice it's one of the most misunderstood concepts in negotiation. People love to invoke fairness when things aren't going their way. But fairness is rarely a fixed point; it's a flexible and subjective narrative shaped by perspective. Is fairness equal risk? Equal reward? Equal effort? Equal access to information? What one party sees as fair, the other may see as outrageous. And this is where many deals derail. People mistake *their* version of fairness for a universal truth.

Smart negotiators know better. They don't chase fairness as a finish line. They treat it as a psychological lens—something to understand and integrate, not argue against. They use it to reveal what matters most to the other side. And when you do that—when you listen more than you speak, when you seek clarity instead of control, when you treat resistance as data instead of defiance, you move the conversation from a stalemate to a solution.

The Art of Strategic Empathy

Over the years, especially as a woman in an industry that was male dominated, I learned that strategic empathy begins with shifting your mindset from proving a point to gathering insight. It's not about being agreeable or soft, nor is it about pushing your way in and demanding a seat at the table. It's about listening for leverage, collecting emotional intelligence, and managing resistance without triggering defensiveness.

Here's how to do it:

1. Start with calibrated questions.

Asking open-ended, pressure-free questions forces people to reveal what they care about most. I often begin with something like, "How do you see us moving forward without compromising on these priorities?" A question like that disrupts the usual pattern of defensiveness. It signals that you're here to collaborate, not dominate, and transforms the energy from opposition to alignment.

2. Use no-oriented questions to lower defenses.

One of the most surprising shifts I experienced came in a heated negotiation with a C-level executive. Every offer I presented was met with resistance. So I asked, "Are you against exploring alternatives that could solve this issue?" The brilliance of this approach is that it gives them a sense of control. Saying no feels safer than saying yes—but in this case their no led to an unexpected pivot. They opened up and even suggested a compromise that supported my objectives. That moment solidified something for me: a no is often the first honest step toward a real yes.

3. Neutralize objections before they surface with an Accusation Audit™.

When I sense defensiveness, I lead with what the other party might already be thinking. "You might assume I'm here to push an agenda, but my priority is finding a solution that works for both sides." That kind of empathy disarms tension and builds trust. It also reframes the entire conversation. Pair this with a calibrated follow-up such as, "What would it take for us to find a way forward that makes sense for both of us?" and you're no longer negotiating positions—you're cocreating solutions. Resistance loses its power when it's named out loud.

4. Label and listen.

There's a perception—especially among men who've been conditioned to view negotiation as a game of dominance—that the loudest, most aggressive person wins. I've learned not to match that aggression. Instead, I observe. I listen. I label what I hear. "It seems like you're more concerned about long-term risk than short-term cost." Simple, but powerful. When you label someone's emotion accurately, it signals respect—and instantly shifts the dynamic.

5. Reframe dominance as data collection.

Years ago in a negotiation with a major tech firm, it initially felt as if empathy would be interpreted as weakness. But I flipped the script and treated empathy as a method of intelligence gathering. I used what I call a Proof of Life™ question: "Are you just exploring options, or is solving this a priority for you right now?" That one question revealed their actual level of commitment and opened up leverage I hadn't seen before. It was a reminder that dominance doesn't need to be challenged; it needs to be decoded. The more aggressively someone pushes, the more information they tend to reveal. When you stop taking it personally and start treating it as data, everything changes.

Empathy is *intel*. It's about mapping the other side's mindset so clearly that you can anticipate, redirect, and lead. Tactical empathy has fundamentally changed how I approach negotiations. It's helped me shift from managing resistance to *understanding* it, and that understanding has led to higher success rates, more collaborative partnerships, and less emotional fatigue. Strategic empathy isn't the soft approach. It's the *smart* one.

Looking back, I've been fortunate to stand on the shoulders of brilliant mentors. They showed me that negotiation isn't about having the loudest voice or the sharpest logic—it's about understanding people. It's about using that understanding to guide them toward a decision they can live with, even if it wasn't their idea to begin with. Time and time again, I've seen deals succeed and fail, not on spreadsheets, but on subtext. I've watched logic fall flat when it couldn't breach the threshold of fear. I've seen dominance provoke silence, rather than cooperation. And I've learned—often the hard way—that people don't resist the deal on the table. They resist being misunderstood, cornered, or rushed.

The real turning point came when I stopped fixating on what I wanted to win and turned my attention to what the other side was afraid of losing. In the end resistance isn't an opponent. It's your invitation. It's a signal that something sacred is at stake, and if you listen closely enough, it will tell you exactly where the leverage lives, where the healing begins, and where the deal can finally move forward.

Winning a negotiation is not about forcing agreement. It's about creating alignment—one question, one moment of patience, one carefully revealed truth at a time.

About Rebecca

For over two decades Rebecca Tedder has helped entrepreneurs, companies, and executives unlock their full potential by bridging strategy, operations, and human capital with behavioral insight, advanced communication, and high-stakes negotiation. Backed by Ivy League credentials and advanced degrees in business and psychology, she offers a rare blend of expertise and execution across M&A and communication strategy as a resolution facilitator and resilience builder.

A growth strategist, behavioral psyops expert, published author, and sought-after speaker, Rebecca has led initiatives that drive measurable outcomes across industries. She specializes in building scalable infrastructures that turn resistance into resilience and bold visions into operational clarity. Her work has helped public and private companies increase revenue, optimize leadership, reduce burnout, and scale with alignment.

Rebecca has partnered in and founded multiple ventures, including *Human Upgrade Media, Access Country, and Axis Advisors*—entities that empower high-performing professionals to rewire for impact, lead with clarity, and scale confidently. One of her current initiatives includes an M&A and a roll-up incubator designed to support founder-led businesses preparing for transformative growth and private equity exit.

She is a respected voice in communication, leadership, and organizational evolution, having spoken at national and international conferences, growth summits, and leadership forums. Leading publications have featured her insights and research on negotiation, advanced communication, resilience, digital transformation, and AI integration. Rebecca actively collaborates with accelerator labs and global thought leaders to support early- to mid-stage teams navigating growth, change, and complexity.

When she's not advising companies or speaking on stage, Rebecca enjoys studying human high-performance, biohacking, resilience, genetics, and antiaging. She also travels, champions charitable causes close to her heart, and spends time with loved ones—including her cherished Havanese, Snugsy.

Learn more:
IG: @TheInstaRebecca
HumanUpgradeMedia.com

CHAPTER 21

SEE, ADAPT, DOMINATE

How to Win in Life

By Rainer Schorr

I stared at the financial report in front of me, my stomach churning. I didn't want to believe what the numbers were showing. Deep down I had known that things were going downhill, but things had gotten so bad I could no longer ignore them. The writing was on the wall. If I stayed in this relationship, I'd be bankrupt in two years.

I had met my girlfriend five years earlier, but in those five years love had twisted into something toxic and unrecognizable. I didn't see it for what it was at first. She needed me, and I was the guy who didn't quit. That's what I told myself as her instability worsened. But the truth is, I was exhausted. Completely drained. If life gives you one hundred units of energy a week, I'd burn through all of mine by Tuesday, pouring everything I had into trying to make her happy and leaving nothing for my business or myself. I was running on empty, and my bank account was the proof. That day, looking at the hard data, I had a choice: sink or cut the weight. I broke up with her.

And suddenly I could see clearly. Not just the financial damage but the real issue—I had been blind to the warning signs. That moment changed me. Never again would I let my compassion betray me or my ambition be sidelined by denial. From that day forward, I paid attention—to my finances, my energy, and my goals. I devoured the right books, rebuilt my mindset, and sharpened my vision. Most people think empathy is about being nice.

But real empathy isn't about kindness—it's about attention. If you look up synonyms for the word *empathy*, you'll find words like "identification," "responsiveness," and "awareness." Tactical empathy is about seeing the game for what it is. And my biggest mistake? I wasn't paying attention—to myself, to my ambitions, to the red flags waving right in front of me.

Since that experience I met and married the most beautiful woman, and we built an extraordinary life together. I build businesses beyond my wildest expectations. Why? Because now I pay attention. When you learn to truly see, anticipate, and respond, that's when you stop sinking and start *dominating*.

The Four Pillars of Success

Everybody wants the secret to making it big when the blueprint has been in front of us for over a century. Wallace Wattles wrote *The Science of Getting Rich* in 1908. Every success book since—*Think and Grow Rich*, *The Magic of Thinking Big*, *The Secret*—pulls from the same foundation. Yet people still get it wrong. They read, they highlight, they nod along—and then they stay stuck. Because reading about wealth isn't the same as building it.

If you want more—whether that means winning a Nobel Prize, becoming an extraordinary parent, or turning into the richest person in your city—you need one thing above all: a relentless commitment to expanding your ambition. Success isn't random. It follows a system, and that system is built on four unshakable pillars:

1. Determination—The ability to push through when everyone else quits.

2. Vision—Seeing beyond your current reality and aiming higher than your circumstances.

3. Self-Trust—The discipline to back yourself and know that you can figure anything out.

4. Gratitude—Not passive thankfulness but active recognition of what you have—and what's possible.

Most people fail because they don't balance these pillars. They chase money but neglect their health. They build empires but wreck their personal lives. Or worse—they play too small, set their ambitions too low, and wake up one day drowning in regret. Yet, the biggest mistake isn't a tactical one—it's a mental one. They confuse obstacles with dead ends instead of seeing them for what they are: opportunities. Two people can stare at the same bankruptcy papers. One sees disaster. The other? A fresh start. Same situation, same numbers. The only difference? Perspective. Solutions never exist at the level of the problem. If you're stuck, you don't need a new answer, you need a higher perspective.

THE FIRST PILLAR: DETERMINATION

The most challenging negotiation I ever faced wasn't about numbers—it was about control. I was preparing for a capital increase with a sovereign wealth fund from the Middle East. On paper, it seemed like the perfect move to strengthen the company's financial foundation. But as the negotiations unfolded, I saw the trap: the terms they proposed would strip me of decision-making power. If I signed, I wouldn't just lose equity—I'd lose control of the company I built.

One wrong move, and I'd fall. The pressure was suffocating, but hesitation wasn't an option. I had to flip the script—to shift from defense to offense, not just to salvage the deal, but to do it on my terms.

The breaking point came when I had to tell both the minister of finance and the CEO of the sovereign wealth fund that I couldn't accept their terms. In the Arab world, that kind of rejection is a high-risk move. The atmosphere shifted. I had just weakened my position instead of strengthening it and I had to adapt—fast.

Instead of focusing on why their offer was unacceptable, I reframed the negotiation. I acknowledged their priorities, respected their vision, and positioned my counteroffer as a path to mutual success. This shift—from confrontation to alignment—changed everything. Empathy felt like a gamble, but determination isn't about bulldozing through obstacles. It's knowing when to push, when to pivot, and when to stand firm. Because in the moments that define your future, the ability to hold your ground while demonstrating empathy is what separates those who control their destiny from those who surrender it.

THE SECOND PILLAR: VISION

One of the most unexpected outcomes I achieved came from a moment of strategic desperation. The terms proposed by the sovereign wealth fund were simply unacceptable, yet rejecting them outright would have put me in an even weaker position. Instead of rejecting the sovereign wealth fund's terms outright, I created leverage. I secured an IPO contract with JP Morgan, even though the IPO was still far on the horizon. This changed everything. Now, I wasn't just a company seeking capital, I was a company with a clear alternative path. The moment they saw the IPO contract, the dynamic flipped. I wasn't at their mercy anymore.

Instead of dictating terms, they adjusted, and it became a textbook example of how reframing the playing field transforms negotiations.

Here's the truth: Most people don't lose because they lack intelligence or talent. They lose because they see obstacles as dead ends instead of puzzles that need a higher level of thinking to solve. The best negotiators don't just find exits—they create new doors.

When you're backed into a corner, don't just look for a way out—look for a way up. How can you reframe the situation? How can you introduce a new variable that shifts the entire dynamic? Every problem has a solution—but it never exists at the level of the problem. You have to rise above it, see around it, and think bigger than the situation you're in. And when you do? You've got the leverage, and you control the game.

The Third Pillar: Self-Trust

Sometimes the hardest task isn't convincing others—it's trusting yourself when your position is challenged. It's easy to spot someone who doesn't trust themselves. They constantly look for external validation and seek confirmation from others. The more you do that, the more you weaken your instincts. If you take fifteen minutes just to decide what to order at a restaurant, you don't trust yourself. And if you can't trust yourself, why should anyone else?

For me, the resistance came from within my own team. During negotiations with the sovereign wealth fund, my advisors told me that showing too much empathy—aligning with the Minister and CEO's concerns—would be seen as weakness. They wanted me to push back aggressively.

But I knew better.

Relationships weren't just important in this culture, they were everything. A direct confrontation would have shattered the negotiation. Instead of dismissing my team's concerns, I explained that empathy wasn't about conceding but about controlling the direction of the conversation. By understanding the other side's fears and motivations, I could steer the conversation rather than react to it.

The evidence came when I secured the IPO contract with JP Morgan. Suddenly, the entire power dynamic shifted. The same team members who had doubted my approach now saw how empathy wasn't about being soft, but about creating leverage the other side couldn't ignore. I had engineered an alternative path, forcing the sovereign wealth fund to compete.

Tactical empathy isn't just about making negotiations smoother—it's about creating leverage where none seems to exist. With the IPO agreement in hand, my company's valuation was already higher than the sovereign wealth fund's initial offer, but the real breakthrough came when the fund adjusted its terms to match the IPO valuation. This gave me an unexpected opportunity. I went back to JP Morgan and said, "I now have a sovereign wealth fund offering me similar conditions. What else can you do for me?" In a matter of days, I had flipped the negotiation on its head. Instead of being forced to accept whatever was offered, I was now the one dictating the pace.

This experience reinforced one of the most powerful lessons in business and life: Had I bulldozed my way through, the deal would have collapsed. Instead, I used tactical empathy to guide the conversation rather than react to it. And it worked.

The Fourth Pillar: Gratitude

Gratitude and ambition might seem like opposites. One teaches us to be content; the other demands more. But they are two sides of the same equation. True ambition isn't just about wanting more—it's about recognizing that opportunity is everywhere, that wealth is not reserved for the few, and that the only limits are the ones you accept. Wealth—whether financial, personal, or emotional—is a function of the four pillars. Determination, vision, self-trust, and *gratitude*—not just passive gratitude, but an active mental state that allows you to see the entire universe as a source of endless opportunity. Every challenge is a pivot point. Every setback, an invitation to think bigger.

Most people ask for too little. They think small, so they stay small. When you ask for more and think bigger, the universe responds. But here's the catch: your results will only ever be as big as your vision. If your ambition is to be the only person in your town driving a Mercedes, that's fine—you'll get there. But if your ambition is to become the next Richard Branson, the work required is the same. The same twelve-hour days. The same strategic decisions. The only difference is that Branson asked for more. I learned that every defining moment—every negotiation, every personal challenge—was an opportunity to shift my thinking. My businesses, my wealth and even my marriage were built on these principles. That, perhaps, is the most powerful lesson I've learned: every obstacle carries within it an opportunity of equal or even greater strength. The challenge is not to focus on the problem itself, but to elevate your perspective and recognize the hidden advantage within it.

You have to step onto a higher plane and ask yourself, "Am I investing my energy into the problem, or am I channeling it into the opportunity this problem creates?"

The amount of energy required is the same. The outcome, however, is radically different.

In negotiations, as in life, the key to flipping the script is understanding that adversity is not an end point—it's a gateway. Once you embrace this, you stop fighting problems and start leveraging them to create breakthroughs. The only real question is, What are you truly asking for?—because the universe doesn't just reward hard work. It rewards the size of your vision.

About Rainer

Visionary Real Estate Developer, Serial Entrepreneur, and Strategic Leader

Rainer Schorr is a distinguished capital market and real estate expert with over forty years of experience in real estate development, fund management, and M&A. With a track record of delivering developments valued at over €7 billion across more than one thousand projects, including five hundred properties in Berlin, he is recognized as one of Europe's leading figures in the real estate industry.

As cofounder and principal shareholder of Standard Land S.A., Rainer leads a consortium of top-tier entrepreneurs and executives from Germany, Switzerland, and beyond. His leadership has been instrumental in managing large-scale real estate portfolios and successfully executing over twenty-five closed-end real estate funds in Germany.

Key Achievements

Serial entrepreneur: Founded multiple successful companies, including DLE Group AG, SIAG Schorr Immobilien AG, GxP German Properties AG, and Accentro Real Estate AG.

IPO experience: Successfully led four companies to public listings, showcasing expertise in scaling businesses to market leadership.

Strategic M&A leader: Oversaw acquisitions of key entities such as B&V Denkmalbauten, Germany's largest developer for heritage properties.

Vision and Social Impact

Rainer's entrepreneurial approach is deeply rooted in sustainability and social responsibility, ensuring projects deliver value not only economically but also socially. His commitment to innovative and eco-conscious real estate solutions is exemplified by the work of DLE Group AG, Europe's second-largest landbank manager.

He is also the founder of GUT ZU TUN, a transformative initiative supported by the European Social Fund, which has helped over five hundred homeless individuals secure employment, training, or education.

> "When people cannot realize their potential, it harms not just themselves but humanity as a whole."

Rainer continues to inspire and lead with a passion for innovation, a commitment to positive change, and an unwavering dedication to social impact.

Learn more:
Standard Land S.A.: www.standard-land.com/de

CHAPTER 22

THE BRIDGE TO GLOBAL EMPATHY

By Sarah Clayton

S he was still on fire when they found her.

Her name was Phoebe—a two-month-old puppy whose body had somehow endured two days of torture. Stoned, beaten, hung in a tree, teeth ripped out, and then finally, set on fire. All of it carried out by three small children under the instruction of their father.

The story tore through the streets of Lusaka, leaving many horrified and grieving. How could children do something like this? The question echoed on radio shows, many filled with disbelief and quiet fury.

Yet not everyone shared that sentiment. "It's just a dog," some said. "We don't have food. Who cares about a dog?" I was in Zambia for business when I heard. The local vet knew me well—I had been bringing her injured strays for years. I called her without hesitation.

"Whatever it costs," I said. "I'll cover it." The vet had never seen anything like it. Despite being nearly burned to death and almost every bone in her body being broken, Phoebe's tail still gave small hopeful wags, a flicker of love from a puppy who had every reason to hate.

As Phoebe's story spread through the community, I began to hear the murmurings: Why the fuss? Why is this *outsider* so worked up over a dog? I was stunned. It wasn't just apathy—it was something colder. A quiet, practiced detachment. The collective shrug of a generation that had grown numb to the suffering of others. Not only could they tolerate it—they had learned to see it as *normal.*

When the police investigated, they uncovered something even more chilling: a belief rooted in superstition. The father's conviction? Phoebe had cursed his newborn child, so he ordered his children to take the puppy into the bush and "finish her." He was arrested, convicted and served three months in prison. The children, still so young, were educated by law enforcement officers who cared. And I was left with questions that would haunt me. What makes it *possible* for a child to carry out this kind of violence? What is the *trajectory* of a child who learns so early how to harm, and so little about how to hold?

We're all born with an innate capacity for empathy. It's part of our wiring—the quiet instinct to recognize pain in another and form social bonds. But empathy isn't just a given; it's something that must be nurtured. Through experience, through the development of emotional intelligence, and through the slow shaping of our cognitive and relational capacities, we learn how to connect. How to care. How to carry each other.

Empathy is often forged in suffering, in chaos, in the absence of gentleness. It grows despite pain—like a tree through a crack in the pavement: stubborn, unlikely, miraculous. To hold on to tenderness in a world that offers no blueprint for it is an act of quiet rebellion. To feel anyway, even when there is no safety or reward in it—that is nothing short of heroic. But Phoebe—battered, burned, brutalized—survived. Not just physically, but emotionally, impossibly. She wagged her tail. She welcomed touch. She trusted. Her little body was shattered, but her spirit wasn't. And in that fragile, flickering gesture, those tiny tail wags—I saw something I couldn't look away from. If she could still choose love after what had been done to her, then maybe so could we. Maybe empathy is less about where you come from, and more about what you decide to protect within yourself. Maybe it's not just born in the trenches—but in what we dare to carry out of them.

I think about the children who hurt her. What stories were

they born into? What hands raised them? What did they see behind closed doors? I don't excuse it—but I can't ignore it either. Children don't invent cruelty. It's taught. Modeled. Passed down. And unless something, or someone, interrupts that cycle, they'll carry it forward. Just like trauma. Just like silence.

Phoebe became a mirror. In her, I saw both the worst we can do—and the best we can still become. Maybe this was never just about saving a dog. Maybe it's about what we're willing to feel and see, and whether we still believe in healing, even when the world tells us not to.

TURNING PAIN INTO PURPOSE

I was still a child in the dying days of apartheid—referendum posters screaming "Vote YES" papered the walls of our garage. I remember watching Nelson Mandela walk free, sitting cross-legged on the floor with other kids, eyes fixed on the television. We understood more of that moment than our age should have allowed. The weight of it pressed into our small chests, even though we didn't yet have the language for what we were feeling. The air was thick—our parents silent, their eyes wet, grief and hope sitting side by side.

The collective pain of our country was raw. The wounds weren't just deep—they were our new foundation. Etched into our homes, our identities, our voices—the fabric of who we were and who we were to become. We were a generation raised on contradictions: born at the dawn of freedom but shaped by the shadows of trauma too vast to name.

My own home was a mirror of these inherited wounds. I was the new generation bound to a cycle of trauma and fractured minds. I inherited a legacy built on survival—a lineage where we never learned to how to break the cycles, only how to live within them. A grandmother who disappeared into silence, a father who returned from hospitals with pieces of himself missing, a mother unravelling under the weight of motherhood, surrounded by whispers and suspicion. And when the fear came—when questions began to surface—it became impossible to untangle what was cause, what was effect, and what was perhaps a cry for help no one knew how to hear. And yet, for the next few decades, my privilege dressed it all in normalcy.

From the outside everything appeared intact. But beneath the surface I was stitching together a life with the only tools I had: hypervigilance, perfectionism, emotional withdrawal, a hunger for connection. I became skilled at scanning rooms for danger, anticipating needs before they were spoken, bending myself to hold fragile dynamics in place. I gave silence meaning and drew logic from chaos. These were not quirks, they were survival strategies. Meticulously practiced. Invisible. Exhausting.

I learned how to brace before I ever understood what it meant to be safe. I became high-functioning in the way that only children of chaos do—grasping for control in a world that had never felt stable, never felt mine. And beneath it all, a quiet grief simmered: for the love I needed, for the child I couldn't be, for the safety I never got to feel.

SEARCHING FOR THE STORY

To truly understand empathy—or its absence—you have to walk into discomfort, bury your judgment and sit with your dissonance. The children who tortured Phoebe were just six, eight, and twelve. It's easier to label them monsters. But violence is learned. Apathy is inherited. And to change the outcome, we have to be brave enough to ask, "What happened to them? And maybe more importantly, what didn't?"

Solving problems begins with understanding—and that requires emotional intelligence, the heart of empathy. Phoebe's story wasn't an anomaly; it was the outcome of a community shaped by poverty, where detachment was a survival mechanism and suffering had become ordinary. To make sense of it, I had to hold space for both my rage and my responsibility. I had to imagine *their* world.

I began listening—really listening—to people's stories. Not to judge, but to connect. Because each conversation isn't just with the person in front of you—it's with a lifetime of pain, belief, and experience. And empathy is the only path that shifts the trajectory of conversations.

One day, a community elder who had dismissed the attack as "just children playing" shared that he was once beaten for crying over an injured animal. His voice cracked as he spoke. In that moment, the story changed. He wasn't outside it anymore, he was inside it. The community was beginning to see itself in the mirror. That moment was a revelation. It showed me that change doesn't come from blame—it comes from understanding. From witnessing. From daring to enter each other's stories.

In 2021 I launched The Global Empathy Project with one belief: Empathy can be taught, modeled, and practiced. It can be *scaled*. We work in places where its absence has caused harm, embedding empathy into real-world interventions that reach both children and adults. Our work interrupts apathy and disconnection, making space for emotional awareness to take root.

What started as a response to cruelty became a mission to scale compassion—to place empathy at the heart of education, leadership, and healing. Through storytelling, dialogue, and lived experiences, we help people not just imagine what it's like to be someone else—but to feel it, stand beside it and respond from that place.

Because empathy is not passive. It's an active, disruptive force. When we meet in that shared space of humanity—not to fix or pity, but to witness—we begin to write a different script, a different future.

THE IMMERSION—SCALING EMPATHY THROUGH EXPERIENCE

Rhinos have walked this earth for over fifty million years—ancient, majestic, and otherworldly. And yet within our lifetime they could vanish. Several subspecies have already gone extinct. Others, such as the northern white rhino, survive only through artificial means, functionally extinct in the wild. Fewer than twenty-seven thousand rhinos remain, and they are disappearing fast.

The reason? Greed. And myth.

Across parts of Africa and Asia, a black market thrives on the demand for rhino horn—a demand rooted not in need, but in fiction. Rhino horn is composed entirely of keratin, the same material found in human fingernails and hair. It holds no medicinal value. Yet, it is falsely believed to cure everything from cancer to hangovers, used as a status symbol, an aphrodisiac, or a show of wealth. These myths, fed by superstition and exploited by criminal syndicates, have made rhino horn worth more than gold—fetching prices upwards of $60,000 per kilogram.

So the poachers kill them. They shoot rhinos, hack off their horns—sometimes while they're still alive—and leave them to die in agony. Many are impoverished locals, drawn in by crime syndicates and fueled by desperation. Some undergo rituals led by witch doctors, meant to make them invisible to law enforcement or invincible in the bush. These practices reflect more than superstition; they are born from desperation. In places where life feels unstable and powerless, people reach for any illusion of control—even if it means surrendering their own power to myth.

The violence is staggering. The brutality, almost beyond comprehension.

To help protect what remains, we launched a relocation program—moving rhinos into highly protected areas to create safe breeding pockets. But this work was never just about moving animals. It was about moving hearts. Because we protect what we love. Many communities living alongside wildlife have never truly seen it. Fenced out of reserves, they've known wild animals only as threats or food—creatures that trample crops, or spark conflict with armed officials when poached for bush meat. Disconnected from nature, it's easy to feel nothing for its loss. So we began bringing people in. Sometimes by helicopter, sometimes on foot, they'd watch as a rhino was sedated for relocation or medical care.

They'd see experts dehorn it to reduce poaching risk, or fit AI collars for tracking. And then—something sacred: a moment when they could walk up to the rhino, place their hands on its side, rest their foreheads against its body, and hear its *heartbeat*.

For many, it's the first time they've ever been this close to something so ancient, so vulnerable. And in that stillness—heart to heart—something shifts. That's what empathy looks like when it becomes practice. People leave changed. Not just moved but mobilized. Because once you've felt the heartbeat of what you're trying to save, indifference becomes impossible. The weight of responsibility becomes real. This is the power of tactical empathy— empathy with intention. When it's lived, it becomes scalable. It lets us face what's hardest: broken systems, uncomfortable truths, and the stories we'd rather avoid.

To stop suffering before it starts, we have to understand what created it. Empathy maps the path—through trauma, misinformation, inherited beliefs, and the silence that sustains harm.

Change how people feel, and you change what they do. And when that shifts, everything else can too.

THE RECKONING: LEADING THROUGH EMPATHY

Not only has using tactical empathy shaped the work of The Global Empathy Project—it has reshaped me. Again and again, I've stood at the edge of incomprehensible cruelty, systemic collapse, and beliefs so deeply rooted they feel immovable. And in those moments, I've had a choice: to meet harm with fury, or to meet it with curiosity.

Empathy doesn't erase the pain. It doesn't excuse the injustice. It creates the space where transformation becomes possible. For me, that transformation has been quiet and ongoing—a slow evolution rather than a singular awakening. I've learned that true influence doesn't come from overpowering someone but from understanding them. Their fear. Their history. Their programming.

In personal interactions I listen longer now. I react less. I sit with discomfort instead of fleeing it. And when I find myself triggered by a situation, I see it not as a setback, but as an invitation—to understand myself more deeply, and in doing so, to heal more fully. That healing becomes the foundation from which I can offer a more nuanced, grounded empathy—even in the face of horror. It has made me a better leader, a better friend, and above all, a better learner of the human experience. Where I once saw unreachable people, I look for the entry point—the fear behind their actions, the truth behind their apathy. Empathy, when embodied, shows us that every resistance has a reason, every harmful act, a wound. And if we're willing to look, we can find that critical point where the cycle might break.

Empathy lets us confront injustice with clarity and courage. It's not optional—it's a leadership imperative, a radical tool for repair. It gives our convictions weight and our strategies humanity. If we want a generation that sees clearly, we must teach them not just to feel—but to feel wisely. Today, Phoebe is alive, healed, and curled beside me on the couch—her gentle eyes watching as I write these words. She is a living reminder that even after unthinkable cruelty, connection is still possible. She chose to trust, to love, to rise. The question is, Will we?

About Sarah

Sarah Clayton is a recognized leader in both humanitarian innovation and smart infrastructure systems. As the founder of The Global Empathy Project, she has dedicated her life to interrupting cycles of trauma, disconnection, and inherited violence across Africa—scaling empathy through storytelling, education, and experiential programs. Since 2021 Sarah's work has impacted communities in Zambia, South Africa, and beyond, offering trauma-informed interventions that shift how people connect, heal, and lead.

Through The Global Empathy Project, Sarah has pioneered a range of high-impact initiatives that translate empathy into action. These include school-based programs that teach emotional literacy and resilience, immersive wildlife conservation experiences that foster connection to nature, and community-led dialogues designed to interrupt cycles of violence and inherited trauma.

Whether it's placing youth face-to-face with endangered species to ignite a sense of responsibility, or working with survivors of abuse to rebuild trust and agency, the project's work centers on the power of lived experience to transform hearts, minds, and systems. Each intervention is tailored to the cultural and emotional landscape of the community it serves—making empathy not just a value but a practical, disruptive tool for social change.

She is also the CEO of Clayton Technologies, a leading electronics integration firm specializing in information systems, life-safety, energy management, and smart automation. Under Sarah's leadership, the company delivers high-performance solutions across Africa and is rapidly expanding its presence in the Middle East and Europe—optimizing security and sustainability in modern buildings and infrastructure.

With a leadership style rooted in emotional intelligence and lived experience, Sarah has become a powerful voice in the movement to make empathy a measurable and scalable force for change. Her insights have been featured in numerous international publications and broadcast platforms, where she shares her expertise on trauma, ethical storytelling, and systems transformation.

She continues to speak globally on how to lead with empathy, design for humanity, and embed emotional intelligence into every layer of education, technology, and policy.

When she's not leading teams or speaking on global stages, Sarah enjoys being immersed in nature and spending time with Phoebe, a rescue dog whose story inspired the founding of her empathy work.

Learn more:
www.globalempathy.org
www.claytontechnologies.com
LinkedIn: linkedin.com/in/sarah-clayton-22319630
Instagram: @sarahlovesafrica

CHAPTER 23

RAISING THE DEAD

By Shanyn Kay Stewart

he last thing you expect to do when your father dies in your arms is negotiate with death itself. But that's exactly where I found myself. The third night I dreamed my father was going to die, I couldn't ignore it anymore. I had to see him. My dad lived alone on a small island off the coast of China. When I finally told him about the dreams, he didn't hesitate. "I know," he said calmly. "I won't see you again."

Days later, without paperwork or permission, I crossed a border I wasn't supposed to cross, sneaking into Communist China because my spirit wouldn't let me stay still. When I arrived, the air around him felt thin and shadowed, as though death were already sitting in the room, quietly waiting to take him. I stayed for a few weeks and kept telling myself I was overreacting. We even went to the doctor, who told us my father was in perfect health. But the next day, in the middle of our meal, my father said, "I don't feel so good," and fell face first into his plate.

The sound that left his body in that moment—what they call the death rattle—is not a sound you ever forget. I dragged him to the floor to begin CPR, suddenly aware that I was in the country illegally, knew no one, and had no phone.

My fear started whispering to me, "You don't belong here. You're not enough for this." But I wasn't giving up. We had a rule in my family: *Ohana. Nobody gets left behind.* Not even in death. I ran through his apartment building pounding on doors and begging for help. His friend, who happened to be a cardiologist, came to my aid and continued CPR. He looked me in the eye and said, "I won't let your father die." But death isn't a fair negotiator.

Finally, the ambulance arrived. As I sat in the back with my dad, a memory emerged. I had been a pastor for eight years, and when I left the church, I had met an evangelist who was leading a training session on how to raise the dead. I remembered his words, strange and beautiful prayers. I remembered him speaking in tongues. But mostly I remembered him saying, "I prayed for thousands, but I only raised 311." Those odds were good enough for me. I saw the spirit leave my father's body, and I began to speak life into death, repeating the words of the evangelist. The paramedics were looking at me as if I'd gone mad. Once we arrived at the hospital, the doctors went to work using the paddles but to no avail. He had collapsed at 9 a.m., and by 3 p.m. the hospital was ready to call it. That's when something inside me broke open.

I let out a guttural scream, an otherworldly sound of protest, and that's when we heard it: *Beep...Beep...Beep...* Just like that, he was back. If you'd asked me before that day, I would've told you I knew fear intimately. I was the person who left mail unopened because I assumed it was bad news. I let the phone ring because I couldn't handle what might be waiting on the other end. I survived the slow death of an eighteen-year marriage, thinking maybe small and scared was just the safest way to live.

But something happened when my father's heart started beating again. I realized fear wasn't the enemy I thought it was. It wasn't there to stop me. It was there to teach me. Here I was, the person who was afraid of everything, and yet it never occurred to me to be afraid of bartering with death. The truth is, 99 percent of what we worry about never happens. The other 1 percent? Well, that's when we get the opportunity to decide who we're going to be in the moment.

Today, I am president of Advanced Accounting Tax & Financial Services LLC, and I spend a lot of my time in intimidating high-stakes conversations. Yet even when there are millions of dollars on the line, I'm never afraid. The significance lies not in the events themselves but in the role you choose to play in the unfolding. I realized that the day my father died and came back to life, the fear of doing nothing was greater than the fear of negotiating with death. I had risked being arrested to see him. I had risked sounding crazy to fight for him. And after that, what exactly was there left to be afraid of?

RAISING YOUR COURAGE

They started calling me "the boss" when I was seven years old.

Growing up in my family's concrete business, I learned early on that being in control wasn't just encouraged; it was expected. For a long time I thought that's what leadership was: control. If I could manage the people, the process, the outcome, I'd be safe. The business would be safe. Life would be safe.

But over time I learned that control is an illusion.

We can't always control circumstances, but we *can* control how we show up in those moments that matter most. We can control our state, our energy, and the way we influence the space we step into. And nowhere is that more important than when communication stalls, when a deal starts slipping away, or when a relationship flatlines and we're left standing there, wondering if we should call the time of death or dare to bring it back to life.

I've seen too many people give up on conversations that still had more to say. I've watched teams walk away from negotiations that only needed one more courageous push. And I've felt the weight of my own exhaustion convincing me to let something die simply because I was too tired to keep breathing life into it. But the truth is, there are moments in business—and in life—when you can't afford to quit. You can't assume it's over just because the pulse is faint. You can't let silence convince you it's finished. When something matters, you raise it from the dead. You stay in the game. You find the words. You knock on the door one more time.

And that takes courage.

It's the same kind of courage it takes to walk barefoot across burning coals. Before my first fire walk, I spent hours imagining every way it could go wrong. My mind ran wild with fear of what might happen if I failed and got burned. But standing at the edge of the embers, I realized the fire itself wasn't my real obstacle. The only thing standing between me and the other side was the story I was telling myself about the danger. It wasn't about the fire. It was about my focus and my decision to keep moving forward, even when every part of me wanted to turn back.

That's exactly what it feels like when you're facing stalled communication or a dying opportunity. You hit resistance, and fear tries to take the lead. It whispers that it's over, that it's pointless, that you're foolish to keep trying. And if you aren't careful, you believe it. But fear isn't a signal to stop. It's an invitation to check your state, lean in, and reengage with intention.

The conversations we're most afraid to have are often the ones that hold the most potential. Raising the dead—whether it's a stalled negotiation, a silent room, or a fractured connection—isn't about forcing something to happen. It's about shifting the energy. It's about refusing to let fear be the final word. It's about choosing to walk through the fire instead of standing at the edge, wondering what might have been.

And what I've learned through years of facing those fires is that the growth we want lives on the other side of the steps we're afraid to take. When we master our state, reframe our fear, and stay present in the heat of the moment, we find that we're capable of reviving what was in grave danger of flatlining.

RAISING EMOTIONAL INTELLIGENCE

Not long ago I represented a client during a high-stakes IRS audit—an audit I hadn't prepared the tax returns for but one where the errors were impossible to ignore. The IRS agent leading the case wasn't just thorough; he was signaling control from the start. He refused to meet at my office, insisted my client appear in person, and within minutes of pushback threatened subpoenas.

But in negotiation, threats reveal more than pressure—they expose insecurity. Chris Voss teaches that the language people use is a window into their mindset, and this agent's constant use of "I" told me everything I needed to know.

Recognizing his need for control, I didn't react emotionally. Instead, I adjusted my strategy. In any negotiation, when you listen closely to the words people use, they'll tell you exactly what they're afraid of—and if you can identify that fear, you can navigate the conversation with precision. The real art is knowing when to push, when to listen, and when to raise the dead parts of a stalled conversation before they bury the deal for good.

So when I informed the agent that my client wouldn't be attending the meeting—since I was the one representing him—his immediate reaction was to escalate. "If you can't answer 100 percent of my questions," he said, "I will subpoena you both." In that moment, I saw the full picture. This wasn't just about correcting a return. The agent was under pressure to recover the $3.5 million the IRS believed my client owed, and he wanted to posture early to control the narrative. My job wasn't just to present the facts but to manage the psychology of the negotiation. So I stayed calm, avoided reacting emotionally, and began to gather everything I needed to reframe the conversation. I didn't just build airtight documentation; I humanized my client through every detail—where he went to college, what he studied, how he relied in good faith on a qualified tax professional. I painted a full picture, making it clear that chasing this case any further wasn't just unnecessary—it was a waste of the IRS' time.

In negotiations like these, tactical empathy is everything. The goal isn't to overpower the other side. It's to understand what's driving them and use that insight to guide the conversation out of conflict and into resolution.

When you really listen—when you pay attention to the words people use and the threats they make—they'll reveal exactly what they're afraid of. Once you understand their fears, you can resurrect even the most difficult conversations before they die on the table.

RAISING THE CONNECTION

There's this myth women in business have been sold: that to succeed, we have to toughen up, lead with force, and leave empathy at the door. We're told to speak louder, push harder, and match the aggression we expect to meet on the other side. For years I wrestled with that pressure. I thought strength meant controlling the room, outtalking the opposition, and proving I belonged by being the most dominant presence in the negotiation. But experience taught me something far more valuable: Empathy is not weakness; it is *strategy*.

Empathy doesn't mean backing down or becoming passive. It means reading the room on a deeper level, recognizing what the other person truly needs and positioning yourself to meet those needs in a way that drives the outcome you're after. This became clear to me during the audit. Before I ever stepped into his office, my intuition had painted the picture. I sensed he wasn't just doing his job; he was carrying personal pressure. I had a feeling that he felt undervalued at work and needed a win not just professionally but personally. He didn't just want compliance from me—he needed respect. He needed to feel like the man in the room. So I gave him that. If I hadn't, the connection would have been dead before we even met. I needed this connection to keep breathing. I didn't roll over, but I didn't posture, either. I sat beside him, not across from him. I asked questions. I invited him into problem-solving. When he threw out an impossible demand, I leaned in and quietly asked, "How am I supposed to do that?" He softened and then started solving the problem *for* me. That's the power of strategic empathy.

Had I walked in trying to "be the boss," we would've locked horns, and my client would've paid the price. Instead, I identified his emotional drivers, adjusted my approach, and guided the conversation exactly where it needed to go without triggering his defenses.

What women and anyone else leading a negotiation need to

understand is that empathy is not the opposite of power—it's the *expression* of it.

Empathy is influence, leverage, and the art of seeing what others miss and using it to unlock the doors they're trying to slam shut.

RAISING YOURSELF

What I've learned, again and again, is that the real power in high-stakes situations—whether it's an IRS audit, a broken negotiation, or a business relationship on the verge of collapse—is not in how quickly you react but in how intentionally you choose to respond.

During the audit, I was able to negotiate the balance due from $3.5 million down to roughly $300,000! And I can credit empathy for that win. For a long time my instinct was to meet pressure with pressure. To push back. To assert control. To dominate the room so no one could question my place at the table. Over time I discovered that real leadership comes when you pause long enough to read what's *actually* happening beneath the surface.

In business things die all the time. Deals stall. Conversations shut down. Trust erodes. People retreat. And the average person walks away, assuming it's over. But I've learned that what looks dead is often just waiting for someone bold enough to revive it. Someone who can hold the tension, listen deeply, and lead everyone back to the table. When you learn how to revive something—whether it's in an audit, a negotiation, or a conversation you thought was over—you realize the same courage that carries you across the fire is what carries you through every challenge you face. And from that moment on, fear loses its power.

You stop worrying about what might die because now you know—you have the power to be the oxygen. You are the one to lead the charge, to keep the machines running, and to breathe life back into connections. If you trust yourself enough, you can raise the bar, raise the game, and ultimately raise the dead.

About Shanyn

Shanyn Kay Stewart is a dynamic author, nationally recognized tax strategist, and trusted adviser to business owners seeking to build legacy and wealth. With a passion for helping entrepreneurs legally pay the least amount of taxes possible, Shanyn has spent decades guiding clients through complex tax planning, business growth strategies, and wealth preservation techniques. Her expertise has made her a sought-after voice in the areas of financial transformation, strategic tax design, and entrepreneurial mindset.

Before stepping into the financial world and becoming an IRS Enrolled Agent, Shanyn served as an American Baptist pastor. Her background in ministry infuses her work with deep compassion, spiritual insight, and a powerful sense of purpose. She brings a unique blend of faith, intuition, and fierce practicality to everything she does—helping business owners navigate both the seen and unseen aspects of success.

Known as a "gun-toting, tactically trained badass," Shanyn is far from your average accountant. She is a transformational leader who believes that success begins with belief, and that mindset, strategy, and faith must work together to create meaningful results.

Through her writing, speaking, and coaching, Shanyn inspires readers and audiences alike to reframe challenges, embrace purpose, and take bold action toward their highest vision. Her debut book, *Raising the Dead*, weaves together storytelling, spiritual truth, and business acumen to help readers discover the life and leadership they were meant for.

Whether she's leading a tax-strategy session or mentoring a new generation of entrepreneurs, Shanyn's mission is clear: to help others rise, thrive, and lead from a place of deep alignment and unshakable purpose.

She currently resides in Michigan, where she balances her business empire, writing career, and speaking engagements with a deep love for her family, travel, and continuing to live boldly.

Connect with Shanyn Stewart:

Email: support@advancedaccounting.com
Website: www.advancedaccounting.com
Website: www.shanynstewart.com